FAST FACTS™
ON
JEHOVAH'S
WITNESSES

John Ankerberg
& John Weldon

HARVEST HOUSE™ PUBLISHERS

EUGENE, OREGON

Cover by Terry Dugan Design, Minneapolis, Minnesota

Harvest House Publishers, Inc., is the exclusive licensee of the trademark, FAST FACTS.

FAST FACTS™ ON JEHOVAH'S WITNESSES

Taken from the *Encyclopedia of Cults and New Religions,* revised and updated.
Copyright © 2003 by John Ankerberg and John Weldon
Published by Harvest House Publishers
Eugene, Oregon 97402

Library of Congress Cataloging-in-Publication Data
    Ankerberg, John, 1945–
        Fast facts on Jehovah's Witnesses / John Ankerberg and John Weldon.
            p. cm.
    Includes bibliographical references.
        ISBN 0-7369-1081-6 (pbk.)
        1. Jehovah's Witnesses—Controversial literature. I. Weldon, John. II. Title.
        BX8526.5 .A552 2003
        289.9'2—dc21   2002013387

Authors' Note

Good literature and further study can be found at www.free-minds.org, which has links to scores of Christian and secular sites that critique Jehovah's Witnesses. Additional documentation for virtually everything in this book is available on the Web, especially at the sites below and their links.

Recommended Reading

David A. Reed, *Answering Jehovah's Witnesses: Subject by Subject* (Grand Rapids, MI: Baker Books, 1996).

Robert M. Bowman Jr., *Jehovah's Witnesses* (Grand Rapids, MI: Zondervan Publishing House, 1995).

Ron Rhodes, *The 10 Most Important Things You Can Say to a Jehovah's Witness* (Eugene, OR: Harvest House Publishers, 2001).

Wilbur Lingle, *Approaching Jehovah's Witnesses in Love: How to Witness Effectively Without Arguing* (Fort Washington, PA: Christian Literature Crusade, 1995).

Randall Watters, *Thus Saith Jehovah's Witnesses: 120 Years of Revealing Documents from the Watchtower Bible & Tract Society* (available from Freeminds.org).

Jerry Bergman, *Jehovah's Witnesses: A Comprehensive and Selectively Annotated Bibliography* (Westport, CT: Greenwood Press, 1999).

Edmond Gruss, *Apostles of Denial* (Grand Rapids, MI: Baker Books, 1976).

Raymond Franz, *Crisis of Conscience* (Atlanta: Commentary Press, 2002).

Raymond Franz, *In Search of Christian Freedom* (Atlanta: Commentary Press, 1992).

Websites (see many important links at each site)

Freeminds.org

ApologeticsIndex.org

Aomin.org/Witnesses.html

WatchtowerInformationService.org

Jehovahs-Witness.com

Johnankerberg.org

Exjws.net

Premier1.net/~raines (Ken Raines)

Geocities.com/osarsif/index2.htm ("Research on the Watchtower")

The authors wish to note their indebtedness to Professor Edmond Gruss for much of the original materials no longer published by the Watchtower Society. (It is apparently standing Watchtower Society policy to remove books or revise them when sufficient publicity comes to light documenting their errors; see Gruss, *Apostles of Denial,* p. 261.)

CONTENTS

SECTION I
INTRODUCTION

1. Who Are the Jehovah's Witnesses? 9
2. How Influential Are They? 9
3. How Did the Jehovah's Witnesses Begin? 12
4. How Are the Different "Eras" in Watchtower Society
   History Relevant to Its Truth Claims? 15
5. What Are Some Important Characteristics of the Watchtower
   Society That Help One Understand This Religion? 19

SECTION II
THEOLOGY

6. What Do Jehovah's Witnesses Teach About Christianity? 31
7. What Do Jehovah's Witnesses Teach About the Bible? 36
8. What Do Jehovah's Witnesses Teach About God
   and the Trinity? 40
9. What Do Jehovah's Witnesses Teach About Jesus Christ? 43
10. What Do Jehovah's Witnesses Teach About the Holy Spirit? 49
11. What Do Jehovah's Witnesses Teach About
    Salvation in General? 50
12. What Do Jehovah's Witnesses Teach About
    Salvation by Works? 54
13. Does the Bible Teach Salvation by Good Works? 56
14. Have the Jehovah's Witnesses Made the Biblical
    Doctrine of Salvation Irrelevant to Everyone? 59
15. What Do Jehovah's Witnesses Teach About
    the Atonement of Christ? 61
16. What Do Jehovah's Witnesses Teach About
    Man and the Afterlife? 66
17. Does the Watchtower Society Support the Occult? 69

SECTION III
A CRITIQUE OF THE WATCHTOWER SOCIETY
AND JEHOVAH'S WITNESSES

18. Can the Watchtower Society's *New World
    Translation* Be Trusted? 76

19. What Do Respected Scholars Say About
the *New World Translation*? 80

20. What Are Some Examples of the *New World
Translation* Mistranslation? 83

21. What Does the Watchtower Society Teach Concerning
the Definition and Interpretation of Biblical Prophecy? 106

22. Does the Watchtower Society Clearly Claim
Divine Guidance in Its Prophetic Ministry? 110

23. What Are Some of the False Prophecies Declared
by the Watchtower Society? 113

24. Does the Watchtower Society Now Admit to False Prophecy? ... 126

25. Has the Watchtower Society Made Important
Changes in Its Divine Revelations? 129

26. Can the Watchtower Society Claim Divine Guidance
and Authority When It Misuses Quoted Sources? 140

27. What Are Some Ethical Concerns with
the Watchtower Society? 142

28. What Are Some Tips for Talking with Members? 154

29. A Personal Word to Jehovah's Witnesses 166

   Watchtower Doctrinal Summary 169

   Appendix: Letter of Dr. Julius R. Mantey to
   the Watchtower Society 171

   Notes 175

A person should make sure that his beliefs can be supported by the Scriptures...

—Official Watchtower Society website
www.watchtower.org

It is entirely unsafe for the people to rely upon the words and doctrines of imperfect men.

—Judge Rutherford,
second Watchtower president

Introduction

1

Who Are the Jehovah's Witnesses?

The Jehovah's Witnesses are a religious sect begun by Charles Taze (C.T.) Russell in the late nineteenth century. They are a committed group of people who follow the doctrines and commands of the controlling entity, the Watchtower Society, in Brooklyn, New York. They are perhaps best known for their aggressive brand of door-to-door proselytizing and their cultural and social repudiations. The Witnesses refuse to salute the flag, accept military service, observe holidays (even birthdays), or accept blood transfusions—even at risk of the death of their own children. They are also known for their numerous false predictions of the coming battle of Armageddon.

2

How Influential Are They?

The Jehovah's Witnesses are members of one of the most successful new religions in the twentieth century. A few statistics enable one to appreciate the growth of this organization from a small group of Bible students in 1870. According to the late Dr. Walter Martin, a recognized authority on new religions: "During the years 1942–52, the membership of Jehovah's Witnesses doubled in North America, multiplied fifteen times in South America, twelve times in the Atlantic islands, five times in Asia, seven times in Europe and Africa, and six times in the islands of the Pacific. By 1973 these figures had almost doubled. Such is the evolution of Pastor Russell's 'Zion.' "[1]

Twenty years later the figures had doubled again. As of 2003 there were approximately 6 million "publishers," or active members, plus 4 to 7 million additional interested persons, or inactive members, who attend the yearly April "memorial" service—the Witnesses version of the Lord's Supper. This means that in terms of influence the number of active members only tells half the story. In some respects, the Watchtower Society (WS) begun by C.T. Russell is today just as influential as the LDS or Mormon church begun by Joseph Smith.

Since 1928 the Watchtower printing plant has sent out *billions* of pieces of literature.[2] In 1975 the Watchtower *Yearbook* (p. 32) listed for 1974 a print run of 51,663,097 bound books, 18,239,169 booklets, and almost a half billion *Watchtower* and *Awake!* magazines. The ten billionth piece of literature was reached sometime in 1988 or 1989; the twenty billionth around 2000. Today the WS sponsors millions of Bible studies each month, and followers spend over one billion hours witnessing.[3] There are over 93,000 congregations in some 235 countries.

The two key periodicals, the *Watchtower* and *Awake!*, have a combined yearly circulation of over 40,000,000 in some 200 languages.[4] Watchtower literature as a whole is published in some 230 languages. The circulations of the two Watchtower magazines rival *TV Guide* and *Reader's Digest* and is said to outsell *Time, Newsweek,* and *US News and World Report* combined. Also, possibly 100 million copies of the Watchtower Society's *New World Translation* (NWT) of the Bible are now in some 30 languages, in whole or in part.

Perhaps no other single religious organization uses the printed page so extensively, dwarfing by comparison the majority of other religious bodies, even, it is claimed, the U.S. Catholic Church.[5]

Of course, other ways of looking at this data are less flattering to the Witnesses. In light of such impressive figures, one is surprised at the relatively small number of converts. Edmond Gruss, Professor of Apologetics at the Masters College in Los Angeles, California, and an expert on Jehovah's Witnesses, calculated back in 1992 that to bring one convert to baptism (the final step in becoming a Witness) involved 10 active Witnesses and some 1800 hours of service.[6]

Freeminds.org on the Web ("How Big Is the Watchtower?") estimated ten years later that it took about 15 years for the average "publisher" or active member to make just one convert. Figures released in 2002, based on WS statistics published each January 1 in the *Watchtower* magazine (from 1988–2001), reveal wide variations by country for producing a single convert—from a high of 74 publishers required in Denmark to 5 in Albania, and a high of 17,415 hours of work in Japan to 1636 hours in Moldova (www.jwic.com/stat/htm).

New members are apparently won only with great effort, which, given the Society's isolationist teachings and other problems, is not too surprising.

It is also true that since its inception in the 1880s, there has been a steady exodus of members from the movement.[7] From 1949 to 1973, at least 400,000 baptized Witnesses apparently left the Witnesses and are no longer active members, half the number occurring between 1969 and 1973.[8] From 1970–1979, over 750,000 left the organization or were disfellowshipped, according to former Governing Body board member and Witness leader Raymond Franz, nephew of the fourth WS president, Frederick W. Franz.[9]

Matters have apparently not improved in the subsequent two decades regarding the continuing overall decline in membership figures, in large part due to the authoritarianism, legalism, stress, and even medical hazards resulting from Watchtower doctrines and the negative publicity involved.

In light of such publicity and various internal difficulties, in 2000 there was a shake-up of the WS organization in an attempt to help assure its future. The WS may also be setting the stage for possible gradual doctrinal changes, for example, in blood transfusion policy and prophetic interpretation. Three new corporations were formed: Kingdom Support Services Inc., the Religious Order of Jehovah's Witnesses, and lastly, the Christian Congregation of Jehovah's Witnesses, which will work in conjunction with the Governing Body. There is also apparently a new legal strategy to keep liability lower. For example, if doctrinal change occurs with the blood transfusion issue, one can only guess at the number of lawsuits from surviving relatives of the estimated 9000 people per year who have died from refusal to accept blood transfusions. (Incidentally, that's three times the casualties of the September 11 massacre.)

It should also be noted that even a decade ago, the WS was a very wealthy organization with "a 1992 American income of $1,250,000,000 plus other income from stocks, land, and other sources" (www.premier1.net/~raines/hate.html).

3

HOW DID THE JEHOVAH'S WITNESSES BEGIN?

In examining the history of the WS, we should note the influence of several different religions upon WS doctrine, especially Seventh-day Adventism.

Charles Taze Russell had a church upbringing but eventually became dissatisfied with certain teachings. After a period of agnosticism, he began exploring other religions to see if he could find something more to his liking. Seventh-day Adventism and Christadelphianism (the latter of which rejects the doctrine of the

Trinity as satanic) exerted a marked influence upon him, and they clearly became a source of his theology—in spite of official silence or denials. In *The Chaos of the Cults,* Dr. Van Baalen pointed out: "The origin of the Russell-Rutherford-Knorr theology, especially of its eschatology, lies in Seventh-day Adventism. This was asserted in *The Chaos of the Cults* in 1929, hotly disclaimed by LeRoy E. Froom, and has since then been reaffirmed by Lehman Strauss, F.E. Mayer, and E.G. Gruss."[10] In *The Theology of the Major Sects,* Dr. Gerstner concurs:

> It is quite clear that the Jehovah's Witnesses are an offshoot of the Seventh-day Adventists....As Ferguson observes, "Evidently his [Russell's] youth was dominated by morbid pictures of a sizzling hell, for as a boy he used to go around the city of Pittsburgh every Saturday evening and write signs with chalk on the fences, warning people to attend Church on the following Sabbath that they might escape the ghastly torments of everlasting fire." From this fiery orthodoxy, Russell, when he found himself unable to answer certain questions of a skeptic, passed over into a frigid unbelief. It was then that he met the Seventh-day Adventists, and his faith in Christianity, especially the Second Advent, was restored.[11]

While Russell was heavily influenced by Adventism, he also modified it. Nevertheless, Adventist doctrines in harmony with Jehovah's Witnesses include 1) the rejection of a biblical hell, 2) the rejection of an immortal soul, 3) in part, a works emph[...] in salvation, and 4) a belief that they are the only true re[...] church.*

---

* Insofar as Adventism rejects salvation by grace through faith alone a[...] it cannot be classified as biblical Christianity. Insofar as it accepts [...] nature of God and other key doctrines, it cannot properly be cl[...] cult in the same category as Mormonism and Jehovah's Witne[...] years traditionalists have quashed biblical reform movemen[...] future health subject to doubt.

If one examines the doctrines of the Christadelphians, it seems evident they also exerted a significant influence upon Russell. For example, they express hostility towards the Church, and they deny the Trinity, Jesus' deity, hell, and an immortal soul. They teach a partial atonement, an "end times" restored church, and the necessity of works-salvation.[12] Professor Gruss, a former member of the Witnesses and author of one of the best texts on the Witnesses, *Apostles of Denial,* points out: "It is difficult to understand why the Jehovah's Witnesses do not claim or even mention in their history the Christadelphian movement....It is certain that this group is a definite source of Russellite theology. Except for minor differences, there is almost a word-for-word agreement between the Christadelphian and the Russellite theology in several areas."[13]

Their teachings also bear similarities to some earlier heresies, notably Arianism (which denied Christ's deity) and Socinianism (which denied the Trinity on the basis of reason and held the Holy Spirit to be an influence or energy coming from God). In fact, Professor Gruss discusses the extent of heresy represented by the WS:

> William J. Schnell, a member of the Jehovah's Witnesses for more than thirty years, views the background of Russellite theology as a background of heresies, the Watchtower Society having "succeeded weaving the threads of all former heresies and cults for a New World Society." That this even an understatement, can y of the history of Christian nent, in that Russell and his ted old heresies but created ver appeared before. Russell, ked up such errors as Uni-, Unitarianism, second pro-, and a peculiar method of mixture of Swedenborgian ethods.[14]

At the least, this information suggests that the origin of the Jehovah's Witnesses is not as original and as unique as claimed by the WS.

4

HOW ARE THE DIFFERENT "ERAS" IN WATCHTOWER SOCIETY HISTORY RELEVANT TO ITS TRUTH CLAIMS?

In that the president of the Watchtower Society tends to leave his own particular imprint upon the Society, we may note six particular "eras" to date:

1. Charles T. Russell   (1872–1916)

2. Joseph F. Rutherford   (1917–1942)

3. Nathan H. Knorr   (1942–1977)

4. Frederick W. Franz   (1977–1992)

5. Milton G. Henschel   (1992–2000)

6. Don Adams   (2000–   )

It is noteworthy that when one compares one "era" with another, significant problems emerge with some of God's alleged revelations and divine instructions to the WS. Parts of the Society's theology, prophetic declarations, and practice undergo various changes, as if God had somehow changed His mind on crucial matters that were once inviolate. We will touch on this at various points later, but for now we will present basic information on the three earlier "eras" for illustration and a general idea of the problem. (Randall Watters' *Thus Saith the Governing Body of Jehovah's Witnesses* has presidential era summaries on the first five eras.)

Charles T. Russell

Russell stressed the reconciliation of God and man through the "atonement" of Christ and the coming restoration of all things in the millennial kingdom, the latter becoming a continuous WS theme. Russell's magnum opus was a seven-volume set of writings called *Studies in the Scriptures*. Given its claim to divine revelation, it became a new Bible for the faithful Russellites of his era. Today, however, despite its authoritative claims, it is, somehow, largely neglected. Further, characteristic to all "eras," its theology was typically anti-Christian. For example, Russell's *The Atonement Between God and Man* contains most of his theology including denials of 1) Christ's deity—study III (compare pp. 83–95); 2) the personality of the Holy Spirit—study VIII (compare pp. 165–172); 3) hell and the immortality of the soul—study XII–XIII (compare pp. 301–333); 4) Christ's atonement—study XV–XVI (compare pp. 422–429); and others. (Vol. 5, Dawn Bible Students' Association reprint of the 1886 ed.)

Russell dubbed himself "God's mouthpiece." He claimed that, compared to reading his books, Bible reading was "a waste of time" and that his books would "harmonize...every statement in the Bible."[15] (See indented quote on p. 37.)

Given Russell's claims to divine authority, one would have expected very little changes in his teachings, but this is not what we find; changes began with the very next president.

Joseph F. Rutherford

In the second era (with Rutherford as WS president) many of Russell's distinctive teachings were basically ignored or discarded (though the fundamental theology remained the same), and an emphasis upon the Jehovah of the Old Testament replaced Russell's Christ of the New Testament, a weight that remains today. Rutherford initiated the new name, "Jehovah's Witnesses," and placed more importance on the vindication of God's name than on Russell's heterodox teaching on the atonement. Rutherford also increased the level of attack upon Christianity. He began an open verbal war against the visible segment of the devil's earthly kingdom, the military-political-religious world system. This has also continued to this day, although in milder form.

Under Rutherford's direction the Society became an authoritarian organization within whose ranks dissent was not tolerated, also something that has remained to this day. (For example, according to recently disfellowshipped member William H. Bowen of SilentLambs.org: "Since January, 2001, I have been contacted by over 5,000 people who were molested as Jehovah's Witnesses. I have spoken to hundreds who were threatened with excommunication if they tried to speak out." <www.watch towernews.org/press073102.htm>.)

Rutherford further expanded the use of an allegorical interpretation of the Old Testament, which, again, has continued. Strategically, he stressed the idea of "progressive revelation," which allowed him to shed "new light" on Russell's earlier teachings.

Actually, his idea of progressive revelation was a denial of the Christian concept. Rather than giving new information on dimly revealed doctrines (for example, in the Bible, the doctrine of the Trinity and the doctrine of eternal punishment, while present in the Old Testament, are more fully revealed in the New Testament), Rutherford actually *changed* Russell's divinely revealed truths into errors and taught new concepts and biblical interpretations that forcefully denied earlier ones[16] (compare Critique section). Thus, it was hardly surprising that during Rutherford's "era of changes," literally thousands of faithful Russellites, perceiving a betrayal of Russell and God Himself, left the organization and started some of the two dozen sects of the Jehovah's Witnesses present today. Rutherford had thus rejected Russell's earlier teaching that new light would *not* contradict previous revelation. In 1881 Russell wrote: "New light never extinguishes older light but adds to it....So it is with the light of truth; the true increase is by adding to, not by substituting one for another." (*Watchtower Reprints*, p. 188; B.J. Kotwall and B. Stett, "Flashes of Light," <www.watch towerinformationservice.org/flashes.html>.)

Nathan H. Knorr

The period under Knorr greatly expanded the organization's numbers (105,000 when he began; 2.2 million when he left). Again, new and contrary divine interpretations replaced old ones.[17] Other important changes were made, also justified by "progressive revelation"; for example, the term "religion," once universally condemned as entirely satanic, was now more acceptable. New stress was also placed on training the Jehovah's Witnesses to defend their interpretation of the Bible, which largely accounts for Witnesses' success today among uninformed Christians, within more or less liberal mainline denominations, and among the spiritually searching segments of the general public. Further, their own highly prejudiced translation of the Bible, the *New World Translation,* was produced in 1950, and it became an invaluable asset in Watchtower doctrinal apologetics and witnessing. (See Questions 18–20.) Despite the various changes in interpretation, the *Watchtower* for July 1, 1943 (p. 202), declared, "Nothing is interpreted but the interpretation comes from God and is then published." (B.J. Kotwall and B. Stett, "Flashes of Light," <www.watchtowerinformationservice.org/flashes.html>.)

Under Knorr, literature produced by the WS became anonymous, although it was accepted that it originated from the Watchtower Society leadership. There was also something of a desire to be seen as respectable in a scholarly sense, and a new stress was laid upon recording the group's history.

Frederick W. Franz and Milton G. Henschel

Subsequent presidents Franz and Henschel continued the same tradition of leaving their unique marks upon the Society's beliefs and practices. Franz ruled from 1977–92 and instituted what appear to be certain paranoid-driven policies designed to "keep an eye on" potential troublemakers in the rank and file, with Witnesses reporting infractions of other Witnesses. Milton G. Henschel (1992–2000) presided over an era where the Governing body and not just the president exerted more authority.

There was an effort to appear more "normal," with less rejection of psychiatrists, college education, school sports, holidays, and other matters. Jehovah's Witnesses have the most wealth, property, and followers of their history, although growth slows down to one to two percent. Apparently dozens of breakaway groups began to form in 1996 based in part on the apparent rejection of the "1914 generation" doctrine given in the October 15 and November 1, 1995, *Watchtower*. Henschel resigned in 2000 amidst organizational restructuring.

Don Adams

Adams became the sixth president in October 2000. It's a bit too early still to comment on his leadership.

What is clear from these different "eras" is that, given the considerable doctrinal and other changes throughout WS history, any claim that the WS has been the recipient of a body of immutable divine revelation, or interpretation of Scripture, is entirely without foundation, as we will see.*

5

WHAT ARE SOME IMPORTANT CHARACTERISTICS OF THE WATCHTOWER SOCIETY THAT HELP ONE UNDERSTAND THIS RELIGION?

In this section we will consider some characteristics of the Watchtower Society that will help one to understand this particular religion and that will also be relevant to later discussions. For example, understanding their concept of a dual classification

---

* Anyone interested in a reliable history of Jehovah's Witnesses should not consult their own histories, for as in Mormonism and other groups, they are largely unreliable.[18] Gruss suggests Herbert H. Stroup's *The Jehovah's Witnesses* (a published Ph.D. thesis, 1945); Edgar R. Pike's *Jehovah's Witnesses* (1954); William H. Cumberland's *A History of Jehovah's Witnesses* (unpublished Ph.D. thesis, the State University of Iowa, 1958); J. William Whalen's *Armageddon Around the Corner* (1962); and Timothy White's *A People for His Name: A History of the Jehovah's Witnesses and an Evaluation* (1968).[19] Gruss' text *Apostles of Denial* presents an excellent survey of Witness history.[20]

of the believer is vital to comprehending their doctrines in general, especially as they relate to salvation. Similarly, their claim to divine guidance and inspiration allows us to understand their placing WS literature on equal footing with the Bible. Understanding the rationalistic emphasis of the WS helps one comprehend their rejection of allegedly "unreasonable" doctrines such as the Trinity, hell, and the deity of Christ. Knowing the Society's authoritarianism makes it easier to understand members' absolute submission to Watchtower programs and practices, such as refusing blood transfusions, nonobservance of holidays (Christmas, Easter, and so on), and refusal to read critical literature. Indeed, the average member is quite fearful of Watchtower Society disapproval, because to be cut off from the WS is to be cut off from God and His salvation, leading to eternal annihilation. We shall examine these and other characteristics in turn.

Two Classes of Believers

One cannot fully understand WS literature unless one understands that there are two distinct classes of believers within the Witnesses. Without realizing who a given section of literature is referring to, one may become confused; for example, by assuming that terms like "anointed class" refer to all Jehovah's Witnesses when in fact they do not. The first class, the "anointed class," are the 144,000 specific Jehovah's Witnesses (God's elect), and only they are "born again." This class is explained by the Witness theory that since A.D. 33 Jehovah God has been choosing 144,000 special individuals as a specific class of people to rule with Him in heaven. (No one in Old Testament times can be part of this class because before Christ no one could be "born again.") The 144,000 have different responsibilities, a different way of salvation, and a different destiny than the second class of individuals, which are the "other sheep," the vast majority of Jehovah's Witnesses. So the Witnesses have two distinct classes of believers: the elect 144,000 and all other Jehovah's Witnesses.

The elect are also referred to as the "faithful and discreet slave" of Matthew 24:45 (NWT). Although they number 144,000, their most crucial segment is the small group of leaders of the Watchtower headquarters at Bethel who write and publish the literature of the Society. While they will one day rule in heaven with their elder brother, Jesus, they now rule the "other sheep" here on earth, seeing themselves in a servant role. Concerning Jesus' parable in Matthew 24:45-51, it is said: "Jesus' illustration began fulfillment at his departure in the year 33 C.E., and this composite 'slave' has been existing since then, namely, 'the Israel of God,' the spirit-begotten, anointed congregation of Christ, the membership of which will finally reach 144,000."[21]

It appears that virtually all of the 144,000 have already been selected, so that among the millions of Witnesses today, the average person has virtually no expectation of being one of "the elect." A few may express the "hope" of election, but this seems to be determined by personal conviction. Thus, the vast majority of Witnesses have no desire to be "born again," and they do not expect, or intend, to go to heaven. They expect to live on a "paradise earth" forever, assuming they pass the many future and quite difficult divine tests required of them.

Exclusivism

Since their beginning, Jehovah's Witnesses, like the Mormons and scores of other new religions, have claimed to be the only organization on earth through which God directs His will and purposes. Most importantly, only through the Watchtower Society and its publications can one find the true meaning of the Bible. The WS is "God's sole collective channel for the flow of Biblical truth to men on earth."[22] The Society's exclusivism is perceived in two ways: negatively, as separation from the entire world system—political, military, and religious (the latter being exclusively the "Great Whore Babylon"*); and positively, as being the sole instrument of God's use to achieve His purposes:

---

* The beast of Revelation 13 is the political-military system; the whore Babylon rides on the back of the beast. Many years ago, the whore Babylon was viewed as the political, military, and religious system; today it is exclusively all false (non-WS) religions.

What about those whom Jehovah today calls "my people"? These are commanded to "get out" of modern Babylon the Great before she is destroyed in the coming "great tribulation" foretold by Jesus Christ....Jehovah's dedicated people have gotten out of her since the postwar year of 1919 C.E.* [23]

We belong to NO *earthly organization*....We adhere only to that *heavenly organization*....All the saints now living, or that have lived during this age, belonged to OUR CHURCH ORGANIZATION: such are all ONE Church, and there is NO OTHER recognized by the Lord. Hence any earthly organization which in the least interferes with this union of saints is contrary to the teachings of Scripture and opposed to the Lord's will[24] (emphasis in original).

Again, along with numerous other unbiblical religions (such as traditional Armstrongism, Christian Science, and Mormonism), the WS claims to be a restored remnant of true believers that has been absent on earth for almost 1900 years. "The falling away of Christian leaders from true Christianity to form a 'man of lawlessness' class or system began shortly after the twelve apostles died....The composite lawless man came out into the open and followed his self-exalting, lawless course of conduct. He set himself up as an apostate clergy."[25]

Claim to Divine Inspiration

The WS leadership has always claimed to receive new revelation and divine guidance, including from angels. However, the great number of changes in doctrines, Bible interpretations, ethical guidelines, and failures in prophecy have forced them to admit human fallibility in the reception of such divine guidance. Nevertheless, for all practical purposes, WS membership believes that the Watchtower Society is fully inspired, and members are

---

*The significance of this date is related to the start of the Rutherford era and reflects the year he began his reorganization of God's "theocratic kingdom."

generally unaware of the extensive nature of the problem (see Critique section). One former 20-year member noted that members commonly believe "the idea that the *Watchtower* and *Awake!* magazines are inspired publications....One JW stated to a Christian, 'Your Bible was finished 2000 years ago, but our Bible has 32 pages added to it every week.'"[26]

Watchtower literature provides many examples of claims to divine inspiration and guidance. Volume 7 of Russell's *Studies in the Scriptures* (published posthumously) declares that Russell "said that he could never have written his books himself. It all came from God through the enlightenment of the Holy Spirit."[27] Judge Rutherford said, "[My] speeches do not contain my message, but do contain the expression of Jehovah's purpose which he commands must now be told to the people."[28] And, "It is entirely unsafe for the people to rely upon the words and doctrines of imperfect men."[29] Anthony Hoekema quotes their history, *Jehovah's Witnesses in the Divine Purpose,* 1959, p. 46 (quoting a 1909 *Watchtower* article, p. 371):

> In 1909 certain leaders of study classes were asking that Watch Tower publications should no longer be referred to in their meetings, but only the Bible. Russell himself replied to this suggestion in a Watch Tower article: "This (the suggestion just made) sounded loyal to God's Word; but it was not so. It was merely the effort of those teachers to come between the people of God and the *Divinely provided light upon God's Word.*"[30]

Throughout WS literature, claims are made that their writings are "Christ's message," "God's message," and "God's truth." The *Watchtower* for July 1, 1973, p. 402, stated that for their group "*alone* God's sacred Word the Bible, is not a sealed book" (emphasis added). One may thus trust in the Watchtower Society just as one trusts in God. (Questions 21–23 on WS prophetic speculation document this attitude in more detail.) Note the comments of several former members:

"In retrospect, I can understand how easily we were attracted by this organization that claimed to be the *only* organization on earth guided by God's 'holy spirit,' and the only organization capable of understanding the meaning of the Holy Scriptures (the *Watchtower*, July 1, 1973, p. 402)." "When questions arose, other Watchtower publications were cited as references because it was claimed that the Watchtower Bible and Tract Society was God's 'sole collective channel for the flow of Biblical truth to men on earth' in these last days (the *Watchtower*, July 15, 1960, p. 439). We were taught that we must adhere absolutely to the decisions and scriptural understandings of the Society because God had given it this authority over his people (the *Watchtower*, May 1, 1972, p. 272)." "To gain...eternal life, I was told, certain things were necessary: 1) I should study the Bible diligently, and only through Watchtower publications...."[31]

Authoritarian

Since the WS believes it alone is divinely guided and inspired, dissent is simply not tolerated. Charles S. Braden, author of *These Also Believe*, observes, "Criticism of the decisions or policies of the headquarters group is likely to be labeled as 'Satan-inspired.' "[32] Gerstner, author of *The Theology of the Major Sects*, asserts,

The organization of the Witnesses is utterly authoritarian. Differences of opinion are simply not tolerated. Defectors from the party line are liquidated from the membership....So then, their nominal acceptance of the principle of an authoritative Scripture is vitiated by the practical acceptance of an infallible interpreter. The right of private judgment is, for all practical purposes, done away with, as the Witness bows to the hierarchy, or rather, the one at the head of the hierarchy.[33]

As anyone knows who has talked in depth with a Witness, dissent, criticism, or independent questioning and reading of "unauthorized" literature is not permitted. One may ask the questions, but one may not question the answers. To do so is to invite disfellowship, which, practically speaking, constitutes the rejection of and by Jehovah God. This carries a potential sentence of eternal annihilation at the judgment, and thus is not something to be taken lightly. Again, to reject the Watchtower Society is to reject God. As former ten-year Witness Bill Cetnar observed, "Whatever word comes from the Watchtower is equal to Scripture."[34] In effect, the WS has made biblical literacy dependent upon Jehovah's Witnesses membership.[35] God's "theocratic headquarters" must be accepted in "its every aspect."[36] In fact, responsible members will be careful to "not be so foolish" as to place "their own human reasoning" above the divinely guided pronouncements of the Watchtower Society.[37]

Biased Emphasis on "Reason"

Jehovah's Witnesses claim undying allegiance to the Bible. But it is clear that this allegiance is only to the Bible as interpreted by the Watchtower Society based upon its own premises. For WS leadership, whatever may be "unreasonable" to them is summarily rejected: the Trinity, Christ's deity, eternal punishment, and so on. Paradoxically, members must *not* use their "human reasoning" to question Watchtower Society teachings, but they *must* use it to question non-WS teachings.[38-42] Indeed, members who have tried to reconcile, or "reason out," confusing and conflicting Watchtower Society policies, prophecies, doctrines, and biblical interpretation find themselves in trouble both with reason and the WS.

Organizational Structure

The organizational structure of the Society begins at the top with Jehovah God. He communicates His will and biblical interpretation to the Watchtower upper echelon (the president and his close associates, known as the Governing Body), who then pass it on to others, where it finally reaches the printing presses and is sent out as Watchtower literature. Former member William Cetnar observes,

> President Knorr made a very significant and revealing statement in 1952 after some of the brothers in editorial had argued over a doctrinal matter. He stated, "Brothers, you can argue all you want about it, but when it gets off the sixth floor *it is the truth.*" What he was saying was that once it was in print (the presses were on the sixth floor), it is the truth and we had to stand unitedly behind it. Franz in court admitted the same; however, he did not speak the truth when he said [under oath] there were no differences of opinion....[43]

The literature of the Society is sold by loyal members who meet several times a week in Kingdom Halls, the Watchtower Society's churches. Active members are known as "publishers" because they secure their literature from the WS and offer it to prospective converts. Active members are to witness as much as possible, carefully recording the number of homes visited (an average of ten or more a week)[44] and the number of hours spent in various activities (back calls, Bible studies, and so on). They are assigned certain "territories" and attempt to make at least two calls a year at each house.[45] Two Witnesses usually work together as a team, one often being a beginner.

As in Mormonism, a systematic program exists for winning new members. In the WS, if it is carried through to the sixth step, conversion is usually successful. These steps are:

1. Placing WS literature into the hands of the household.

2. Calling again to encourage the person to read and study the literature, using current events to spark interest. *Awake!* magazine especially is used for this purpose.

3. Starting a weekly home "Bible" study on the literature received. (These are not true Bible studies but studies of

Watchtower Society literature offering its prejudiced interpretation of the Bible.)

4. Inviting the potential convert to an area study group where the person can be engaged in a carefully controlled dialogue with Witnesses.

5. Inviting the prospect to attend a "Watchtower Study" at a Kingdom Hall.

6. Starting the person on a similar program of reaching his neighbors, under Watchtower Society care and guidance.

7. Having the person now in regular attendance at Watchtower Society meetings dedicate himself to God's service through water baptism, which officially makes the person a "minister" of Jehovah and a representative of the Watchtower Society.[46]

The Watchtower Society takes pride in noting the harmony, ethics, and efficiency of its organization, but this is more outward appearance. Indeed, many religions today attempt to justify their questionable or unethical behavior in proselytizing, or other activities, on the basis that it makes converts or offers other benefits. The followers of Sun Myung Moon may engage in "heavenly deception," Hare Krishnas may use "transcendental trickery," and the Family (formerly Children of God) may "plunder the Whore Babylon." The Watchtower Society has "theocratic tact" to sanction its own behavior.

The unfortunate problem with a redefining or suppressing of ethics is that it generally returns to haunt us. In the case of the WS, one usually does not discover the extent of Society problems until one has been a member for several years and has been appointed an elder. Dr. Montague, a 20-year member and current Christian psychiatrist with inside information on the problems of Jehovah's Witnesses (author of *Jehovah's Witnesses and Mental Illness*), informs us that within the organization at all levels there exists a great deal of cover-up, authoritarianism, legalism, selfishness, lack of love, power struggles, personality conflicts, and complaints, and he asserts that such things "are common."[47] This has been confirmed in greater detail by former Watchtower leader Raymond Franz in his enlightening and powerful exposés, *Crisis of Conscience* and *Searching for Christian Freedom*. Nevertheless, Dr. Montague observes that the Society goes to great pains to cover up its unwashed laundry:

> When we look beyond the attractive veneer, we find an endless number of a wide variety of problems rampant both within the typical congregation and the whole Watchtower organization. The J.W.'s are anxious to present a favorable picture of themselves to others because this helps "sell" their organization. And selling the Watchtower Society is an important goal of every J.W. Conversion, in the Witness sense, is actually conversion to accepting the idea that the Watchtower Society is God's channel....The key goal of the Witnesses is to help the J.W. to become loyal to the organization, and once loyalty is achieved, passive consent in all other areas usually follows....Thus the J.W.'s take pains to cover these [problems] up, especially from neophytes....[48]

Montague observes that once a member becomes an elder he discovers even more serious concerns, involving mental problems and, not unexpectedly, serious doubts as to the reliability of the WS:

> The new elder discovers J.W.'s have a large number of problems, including emotional and mental health problems, as well as spiritual problems. There is much unhappiness, restlessness, doubts, and misgivings about the Wt. Society and the Wt. teachings. Further, the fact that a number of Witnesses have been abused by either the Society or its representatives comes to light. As one elder stated after six months in this role, "I never dreamed that Witnesses had so

many problems—I have seen problems almost without end. I never realized a group of people could have so many problems including, and by far not the least common, doubts about the validity of the Wt. teachings."[49]

Montague also notes the ethical dilemma raised by Watchtower operations:

> The fact that these problems are hidden from the typical J.W., and especially newer J.W.'s by concealment, prevarication, and open lying raises ethical problems which could cause one to question the validity of the rest of the teachings of the Wt. Society....Witnesses in high positions generally recognize that this is deceitful, but feel that the ends justify the means....If the person can achieve, according to Witness doctrine, everlasting life, deceiving him in the early stages of conversion, J.W.'s feel, is justified. The Society has openly justified this under the rubric of "theocratic tact" or where it is felt proper to protect "the Wt. organization."[50]

Thus, despite the Watchtower website claim that "the most outstanding mark of true Christians is that they have real love among themselves,"[51] the truth is closer to the sentiments expressed by Dr. Montague: "J.W.'s tend to look out for their own interests, and especially their own ego needs, and are only outwardly concerned about others. Probably the most common complaint among the congregations today is that there is 'a lack of love.' This 'lack of love' is commonly bemoaned among Witnesses everywhere."[52]

In conclusion, as is generally true in the world of new religions claiming compatibility with Christianity, far from being the model of organizational efficiency, inner harmony, and Christian love presented to the world, the reality may be quite different.[53] The granting of divine authority to the WS (without justification) is a fundamental cause of these problems. As in Mormonism, the leadership is biblically untrustworthy and self-serving, if not corrupt, because, as is so often true, absolute power corrupts absolutely. Despite abundant claims to "follow Christian principles" and to "obey Jesus," the words ring hollow given WS history. The kinds of well-researched reports one can find on the Web about WS leadership is proof enough. Practically speaking, in the lives of many devoted members, the Watchtower organization ends up being more important than Christ Himself.[54]

THEOLOGY

6

WHAT DO JEHOVAH'S WITNESSES TEACH ABOUT CHRISTIANITY?

Jehovah's Witnesses claim to be Christian, and this is usually how non-Witnesses view them. For the Watchtower Society, this is all to the good, as a large part of their membership is derived from Christendom in general: Catholics, nominal Protestants, new or immature believers, and so on. Professor Gruss points out some consequences:

> The work of the Witnesses among nominal Christians and new converts has caused the Church of Christ much trouble. With a missionary background, William Kneedler, in his booklet *Christian Answers to Jehovah's Witnesses,* rightly states that their "work is parasitic on established Christian work and very confusing to new Christians and to those not well-grounded in the reasons for their beliefs." It is unfortunate that most Christians and pastors are not sufficiently aware of the Witnesses' history, their doctrines, and their methods to deal intelligently with them.[55]

For the Witnesses, both Catholicism and Protestantism (liberal and conservative) are lumped together historically under the derogatory terms "Christendom" or "Religionists." As in Mormonism, since the beginning the Witnesses have instituted a broad-based attack against Christianity as satanic, pagan, evil, and under the judgment of God. For example, the fervent denunciations against false prophets in the Old Testament are routinely applied to Christian pastors.[56] Numerous researchers have noted this fact of Witness hostility to the Christian Church. Charles S. Braden in *These Also Believe* states, "Toward the churches the Witnesses are quite hostile."[57] Anthony Hoekema, in *The Four Major Cults,* observes, "The attitude of the Jehovah's Witnesses toward the Christian Church in general is so utterly bigoted as to be almost unbelievable."[58] The late Dr. Walter Martin observed, "Reviewing the mass of indictments and undocumented charges against Christendom and the clergy, the Christian cannot help but be shocked at the accusations hurled helter-skelter by the Witnesses."[59]

The WS sees Christendom as militantly engaged in a life or death battle against Jehovah God and against God's true people. Satan's conspiratorial efforts are especially directed against Jehovah's "Theocratic Kingdom." His underlings are organized into two principal divisions: a visible segment (the political-religious-military empire of the world) and an invisible segment (the spirit world of demons). It is hardly surprising that some Jehovah's Witnesses may border on paranoia: Both what they see and what they do not see are seeking their spiritual destruction.

Although the attacks against Christianity have been somewhat toned down, they have never fully let up since the days of Russell and Rutherford. Christianity has been portrayed in the following ways.

Satanic

> The Anglo-American empire system, which chiefly
> is "Christendom," Satan makes his chief spokesman
> on earth, and therefore in the Scriptures this system
> is called the "false prophet"; and by this beastly

organization Satan speaks to and deceives the people....That conspiracy is formed, and the overt acts are committed against God's anointed within the realms of "Christendom," and this is further proof that "Christendom" is Satan's instrument.[60]

Christendom's religion is demonism.[61]

Immoral

In his 1937 book *Enemies,* Judge Rutherford stated, "All liars and murderers are religionists."[62] "In these religious organizations are included thieves, robbers, liars, whoremongers, murderers, manstealers or kidnappers, frauds, cheats...using a great mountain of lies behind which the racketeers hide themselves."[63] The September 1, 1979, *Watchtower* declared: "Today the immoral condition of Christendom is notorious, 'horrible,' on a scale grander than in Sodom and Gomorrah. Deservedly Christendom will suffer the fate of those ancient immoral cities. As the most reprehensible ones among the people of Christendom, the clergy and religious leaders will drink the potion of death."[64]

A wicked persecutor

Christendom's clergy, like Zedekiah and his band of false prophets...have tried to suppress the preaching done by the anointed remnant.[65]

She has been...treacherous....Heartlessly she has despoiled such Christians because they keep the commandments of Jehovah God....Christendom has been foremost in this program of dealing treacherously and despoiling.[66]

The chief component of "Babylon the Great"

Jehovah's Christian witnesses are the ones that have identified who Babylon the Great is....Her blasphemies

exceed those of "pagandom."...Her bloodguilt
exceeds that of all the non-Christian religious realm!
Not out of line with this, Christendom will be given
first attention in the execution of divine judgment
upon Babylon the Great, according to what appears
from the inspired Scriptures.[67]

Hateful to God and His people

Down will come the Devil's agency of religious persecution, Christendom, as utterly rejected by Jehovah
God and Jesus Christ....Up will come Jehovah's per-
secuted witnesses in an overwhelming display of his
choice and approval of them before all heaven and
earth.[68]

By His destruction of Christendom the Sovereign
Lord Jehovah must absolve himself from all responsibility for her shameful course throughout the centuries of her existence.[69]

Inferior to Jehovah's Witnesses

In sharp contrast to Christendom and Judaism,
Jehovah's Christian witnesses, who are residing in the
spiritual paradise of his favor and protection, are the
ones that have taken Jehovah as their King....They
are therefore the ones that are safeguarded from the
spiritual sicknesses and maladies and plagues that
afflict Christendom and Judaism.[70]

The way of death

Christendom's course is "the way of death." Let us go
no farther in it. Time still allows for a person's escape
from being executed with her.[71]

Worthy of death

Today Christendom's clergy-prophets outspokenly
back up the international conspiracy against

Jehovah's kingdom by his Christ. Jehovah's Witnesses are not authorized to pronounce the death sentence upon any of them. But they can take up the inspired utterance of Jehovah and apply it against the clerical false prophets....So, here now let us read of Jeremiah's prophetic actions...."Look! I am sending you away from off the surface of the ground. This year you yourself must die, for you have spoken outright revolt against Jehovah."

—Jeremiah 28:15,16[72]

Jehovah today has not minced words in stating his judicial decision against Christendom. He has commissioned his Jeremiah class [Jehovah's Witnesses] to declare a correspondingly straightforward message of calamity to the modern counterpart of ancient Jerusalem and Judah. Unsparingly, unwaveringly, the Jeremiah class must adhere to all that He commands them in His Word.[73]

Anti-Christ

Ever since the first century the identity of what the apostle Paul called "the son of perdition" or "son of destruction" had puzzled Christians. But in Jehovah's due time this "mystery of iniquity" or "mystery of lawlessness" was scheduled to be unraveled...as an apostate clergy.[74]

The Watchtower Society even alleges that Christianity is "responsible for the physical and spiritual miseries of the poor," that their "pretended interest in the poor is sheer hypocrisy," and that Christianity is also "responsible" for World Wars I and II![75]

Not surprisingly, Christian missionaries often find that the Witnesses have gone ahead of them in many countries. Over the years we have received several letters indicating this, such as the following from a missionary team in Mazatlán, Mexico: "In exploring new areas [Tehuacán and elsewhere], we were astounded at the amount of work the Jehovah's Witnesses have done here. Almost every village we have visited has some Jehovah's Witnesses, and there are areas where entire towns have converted to this cult. Jehovah's Witnesses make conversions doubly difficult."[76]

At the time of publication of this book, the official WS website continued to carry statements like this one from the article, "Christendom Has Betrayed God and the Bible":

> Since its religion came to the forefront in the fourth century, Christendom has proved to be an enemy of God and of the Bible. Yes, the facts of history show that Christendom has betrayed God and the Bible....The fundamental doctrines of Christendom are based not on the Bible but on ancient myths.... No, the nations and churches of Christendom were not, and are not, Christian. They are not God's servants. His inspired Word says of them: "They publicly declare they know God, but they disown him by their works, because they are detestable and disobedient and not approved for good work of any sort"—Titus 1:16....Thus, by what they have taught and what they have done, the religions of Christendom have demonstrated that their claim of believing in the Bible and of being God-fearing and Christian is a lie. They have betrayed God and the Bible (www.watch-tower.org/library/pr/article_04.htm).

7

WHAT DO JEHOVAH'S WITNESSES TEACH ABOUT THE BIBLE?

Jehovah's Witnesses believe that the Bible is the inspired Word of God. However, as noted earlier, they believe only the Watchtower Society can properly interpret it, because only the WS receives divine illumination as to its true meaning. In other words, the Bible is a closed book to all non-Jehovah's Witnesses, who, bereft of God's official interpretation of His word, are incapable of understanding its true teachings. Indeed, apart from WS leadership, it would be a closed book even to ordinary Jehovah's Witnesses. Thus the Bible must be illuminated through its "official interpreter," the WS. WS interpretation could also be said to be a Bible above the Bible, since the Bible we have is, for all practical purposes, useless without it.

In the early days the interpreter was Russell, and then Rutherford; today it is the Watchtower Society as represented by their published literature. In Russell's era, it was stated that his *Studies in the Scriptures* were necessary to comprehend the Bible accurately. In fact, *Studies* were more important than the Bible, for without them the Bible was only a closed book leading to spiritual darkness:

> We might not improperly name the volumes "The Bible in an Arranged Form." That is to say, they are not mere comments on the Bible, but they are practically the Bible itself. Furthermore, not only do we find that people cannot see the divine plan in studying the Bible by itself, but we see, also, that if anyone lays the "Scripture Studies" aside...and ignores them and goes to the Bible alone, though he has understood his Bible for ten years, our experience shows that within two years he goes into darkness. On the other hand, if he had merely read the "Scripture Studies" with their references and had not read a page of the Bible as such, he would be in the light at the end of two years, because he would have the light of the Scriptures.[77]

Since Russell's time, WS publications have occupied the same prominence in the Society as Russell's *Studies in the Scriptures*. No matter how much one studies the Bible, one will end up in spiritual darkness apart from WS publications. As one former member complained, "Real Bible study has been gagged and suppressed by the organization."[78]

Thus, although Jehovah's Witnesses adamantly claim to believe in the Bible as the inspired Word of God, their particular assumptions and false hermeneutical methods force a preconceived theology into its pages.[79] It is not surprising that any number of researchers have noted that the Watchtower Society has an entirely unjustifiable methodology at this point. Dr. Anthony Hoekema categorized four errors of their interpretive methods:

1. Absurd literalism and spiritualizing (for example, Leviticus 17:14 being used to deny blood transfusions);

2. Absurd typology (for example, Noah's wife as a type of the "144,000" elect);

3. "Knight-jump exegesis,"* jumping from one part of the Bible to another in complete disregard of the context in order to "prove" their teachings; and

4. A "rearview method" of prophetic interpretation, or arbitrarily selecting certain events, "aligning" them with a particular Biblical passage, and then claiming "prophetic fulfillment."[80]

As one example of this fourth method, consider their interpretation that the 1918 jailing of Watchtower Society leaders was a fulfillment of Zechariah 13:7, which refers to Jesus Christ and not to Judge Rutherford. This was what was being asserted in 1973.[81] However, in 1933 the same event was being proclaimed as a fulfillment of Daniel 8:9-12, which has nothing to do with the internal events of the Watchtower Society in 1918![82] Hoekema concludes: "Their very method of interpreting the Scriptures makes it impossible for them really to listen to God's Word. Given the methods previously described, one can draw from the Bible virtually any doctrine his imagination can concoct."[83]

---

* An allusion to chess where the knight is able to jump in an "L"-shape fashion, circumventing pieces "in the way."

Professor Gruss points out nine errors of Watchtower hermeneutics, most of which will be illustrated as we proceed:

1. A rationalistic premise that discards "unreasonable" teachings;

2. A concept of "progressive revelation" that changes error to truth and truth to error;

3. An allegorical method whereby the Bible "becomes like putty" in the interpreter's hand;

4. Unwarranted speculation, especially in the area of prophetic chronology;

5. An arbitrary division of biblical contents where certain Scriptures refer only to: a) the "144,000," or b) the "Great Multitude" (the rest of the Witnesses);

6. Ignoring the context; for example, Jeremiah 10:3-4 to teach against Christmas trees and Galatians 4:8-11 to teach against observing holidays;

7. Repeated violation of rules of grammar;

8. Violating word meanings (for example *kolasin* in Matthew 25:46 is translated as "cutting off," not its real meaning of "punishment"; *theotes* in Colossians 2:9 is translated as "divine quality" rather than "fullness of deity"); and

9. Ignoring the tenor of Scripture.[84]

Gruss concludes correctly that the Society's hermeneutics powerfully refute any claim to accept biblical authority. The infallible interpreter is, for all practical purposes, more inspired than the Bible. Thus, as C.T. Russell pointed out, one does not even need to read the Bible, only the literature of its official interpreter. Gruss concluded: "With the methods employed by the Society in interpreting the Scriptures, it really would not matter if the Witnesses held the doctrine of inspiration or not, for the Word of

God is twisted so that the infallible (at the time of the doctrinal pronouncement at least) interpreter is more inspired than the Bible....The Bible has been subordinated to the subjective outlook of the interpreter."[85]

8

WHAT DO JEHOVAH'S WITNESSES TEACH ABOUT GOD AND THE TRINITY?

The Jehovah's Witnesses deviate from the biblical view of God in several important areas. First, God is only one person, not three persons or triune. Second, God is limited to a specific locale and is not omnipresent. Thus the Jehovah's Witnesses' God is "not part of [the] Triune Godhead, with other coequal members."[86] And, "The true God is not omnipresent, for he is spoken of as having a location (1 Kings 8:49; John 16:28; Hebrews 9:24). His throne is in heaven (Isaiah 66:1)."[87] "[God is] not omnipresent, but can project spirit anywhere to accomplish His purpose."[88]

As we will see in our discussion of the Society's position on salvation, it is also true in Watchtower theology that, as far as God is concerned, "the stress appears clearly to lie upon the side of his power and his inexorable justice rather than upon the side of his love and forgiveness."[89] Nevertheless, the Watchtower Society's abhorrence of a "pagan Trinity" makes the Christian God abhorrent to Witnesses. C.T. Russell blasphemously taught that the Christian God was, in fact, the devil: "The clergy's God is plainly not Jehovah but the ancient deity, hoary with the iniquity of the ages—Baal, the Devil Himself."[90]

There are five principal reasons why the Trinity is rejected by the Watchtower Society:

The Trinity was not part of the early church but a development from paganism.

> This doctrine was unknown to the Hebrew prophets and Christian apostles....The early Christians who were taught directly by Jesus Christ did not believe that God is a "Trinity." The trinity is referred to as "that idea of pagan imagination."[91] [However, a study of the earliest church Fathers proves the early Church did believe in the Trinity, because it was clearly the teaching of the New Testament, as documented in our *Knowing the Truth About the Trinity* (Eugene, OR: Harvest House, 1997).]

The Trinity is not found in the Bible.

> Their word "Trinity" does not occur in the Holy Bible.[92] [Lack of a descriptive term does not require the doctrine be absent. Neither does "monotheism," "Jehovah," "theocratic," or "New World Society."]

The Trinity was invented by Satan to malign Jehovah's name and to deceive and confuse people.

> The doctrine of the Trinity is a false doctrine and is promulgated by Satan for the purpose of defaming Jehovah's name.[93]

> The plain truth is that this is another of Satan's attempts to keep God-fearing persons from learning the truth of Jehovah and his Son, Christ Jesus.[94] [If it is biblical teaching, the doctrine can neither be satanic nor malign God's name.]

> There can be no compromise with God's truths. Hence, to worship God on his terms means to reject the Trinity doctrine....God's interests are not served by making him confusing and mysterious. Instead,

the more that people become confused about God and his purposes, the better it suits God's Adversary, Satan the Devil, the "god of this world." It is he who promotes such false doctrines to "blind the minds of unbelievers" (2 Corinthians 4:4). ("Worship God on His Terms," <www.watchtower.org/library/ti/article_09.htm>.)

The Trinity is a doctrine of polytheism, teaching three gods.

If there are three Almighty Ones, how could there be one most mighty?[95]

However, according to Trinity teachers, when "the Word became flesh," Mary became the mother of God. But since they say God is a Trinity, then the Jewish virgin Mary became the mother of merely a third of God, not "the mother of God."[96]

[It is] a bit difficult to love and worship a complicated, freakish-looking, three-headed God.[97] [These are incorrect descriptions or caricatures of the historic doctrine of the Trinity, which teaches belief in one God. We discussed this in *Knowing the Truth About the Trinity*.]

The doctrine of the Trinity "is irrational."[98]

Many things are beyond our full comprehension, such as particle physics. This does not make them irrational.

The extent of WS distortion surrounding the doctrine of the Trinity, even in its more recent scholarly literature, such as Greg Stafford's *Jehovah's Witnesses Defended*, is difficult to imagine for those who have not read it. After analyzing the anti-Trinitarian argumentation in *Let God Be True* (a brief statement of Watchtower beliefs in outline form), Professor Gruss makes the comment: "After starting with no evidence, misrepresenting orthodoxy, using Scripture out of context, not understanding the meaning of a word, misrepresenting the source of the Trinity doctrine, bringing in irrelevant material and changing the events of church history, the Witnesses make this 'authoritative' statement: 'The obvious conclusion is, therefore, that Satan is the originator of the trinity doctrine.'"[99] (For biblical documentation of the Trinity, see pp. 161–62.)

9

WHAT DO JEHOVAH'S WITNESSES TEACH ABOUT JESUS CHRIST?

The Watchtower "Jesus" has existed in three different stages, even, in a sense, as three different persons: 1) the Archangel Michael (also "the Word"), 2) the man Jesus of Nazareth, and 3) a new superior, re-created Archangel Michael.

Clearly, there is believed to be some kind of correspondence between the three; however, the Society's doctrine at this point is confusing. For example, the first person, Michael the Archangel, became Jesus of Nazareth; then this second person, Jesus, became the new Michael. When Jesus of Nazareth came into existence, Michael was no longer, and when Jesus of Nazareth "resurrected" (was re-created, see below) and became a new Michael, Jesus of Nazareth was no longer. It appears from WS writings that the human Jesus was *not* the same person as the prehuman or the posthuman Jesus. The Witnesses are ambiguous at this point, seeming to both affirm and deny interrelationships between the three entities. In light of WS concern with "rational" doctrine, not to mention their consternation with the "confusing" doctrine of the Trinity, we could conclude, because trying to reason out WS Christology really does lead to confusion of mind, that it can't possibly be true. Nevertheless, here are the Society's three, for lack of a better term, "phases" of Jesus.

Jesus as Michael the Archangel (also "the Word")

Scriptural evidence indicates that the name Michael applied to God's Son before he left heaven to become Jesus Christ and also after his return. Michael is the only one said to be the "archangel," meaning "chief angel" or "principal angel."[100]

Michael was the first "spirit-son" of God. He was a direct creation of God (thereby becoming His Son) and finds his uniqueness in that fact. God eventually created other spirit-sons (angels) through this Michael. In heaven Michael was the head of the angels, or the archangel. "However, by virtue of his being the sole direct creation of his Father, the first-born Son was unique, different from all others of God's sons, all of whom were created or begotten by Jehovah through that firstborn Son."[101]

Jesus as a unique man

The Watchtower Society denies the Christian doctrine of the incarnation.[102] They believe that when Jesus was conceived, "Michael" no longer existed: the life force of the person who was Michael was transferred to a female ovum:

Since actual conception took place, it appears that Jehovah God caused an ovum or egg cell in Mary's womb to become fertile, accomplishing this by the transferral of the life of his firstborn Son from the spirit realm to earth (Galatians 4:4). Only in this way could the child eventually born have retained identity as the same person who had resided in heaven as the Word....From the results revealed in the Bible, it would appear that the perfect male life force (causing the conception) canceled out any imperfection existent in Mary's ovum....Since it was God's holy spirit that made the birth possible, Jesus owed his human life to his heavenly Father, not to any man.[103]

As noted, the Society here claims that Jesus "retained identity as the *same* person who had resided in heaven." When Jesus was born, Michael per se ceased to exist as a spirit for "He laid aside completely his spirit existence."[104] "Almighty God divested the Son of his heavenly godlike existence and transferred his life from heaven to Mary's womb."[105] However, not all commentators would agree that Watchtower theology permits a continuity of identity between the preincarnate Michael, the incarnate Jesus, and the new postincarnate Michael. In part this is due to conflicting data in Watchtower theology itself and in part to "Michael's" own transformation from a special but mortal angel to a literal human being to a new, improved, spiritually re-created, and more powerful immortal angel.

Dr. James Bjornstad observes,

> This doctrine reveals a disjointed view of Christ, even though Jehovah's Witnesses seem to portray continuity between the various states of existence. According to the Jehovah's Witnesses, the one who laid down his life at Calvary for our sins was not the one who existed in heaven and had been the Father's agent in creation. Furthermore, he was not the one who was raised from the dead and who now rules in heaven over his kingdom.[106]

Hoekema asks,

> Is there real continuity between the Son of God in his prehuman and his human state? Was the child born of Mary really the same individual who existed previously in heaven as the Archangel Michael? To this question it is difficult to give an unambiguous answer. On the one hand, Jehovah's Witnesses frequently speak of "Christ's prehuman existence," [they] say that the angel Michael was actually Jesus Christ in his prehuman spirit form, and assert that it was God's only-begotten Son who became a man. Other passages from their writings, however, imply

that there was no real continuity between Michael
and the man Jesus Christ.[107]

Nevertheless, the WS claims that when Michael became Jesus
upon the earth, this is when he earned his immortality. "Christ
Jesus was first to receive immortality as a reward for his faithful
course on earth...."[108] "Finishing his earthly course free from flaw
in any sense of the word, Jesus was acknowledged by God as justified. He was thus the only man who, through test, stood firmly
and positively just, or righteous before God on his own
merit....Jesus Christ, after his faithful course until death was
'made alive in the spirit,' given immortality and incorruption."[109]

The WS also teaches Jesus became "the Christ" at his baptism. "As
regards Jesus, according to the angel's announcement at his birth in
Bethlehem he was to become a 'Savior, who is Christ the Lord.' When
did he become Christ or 'Anointed One'? After the prophet John the
son of priest Zechariah baptized Jesus in the Jordan River....Not at
birth, but at thirty years of age Jesus became Christ or 'Anointed
One.'"[110] This contradicts Luke 2:11, which declares that Jesus was
born the Christ. Nevertheless, the Society at this point believes
that Jesus was "born again," becoming the firstborn of all begotten
sons of God.

Jesus as a new improved Michael

According to Jehovah's Witnesses, when Jesus of Nazareth
died, He ceased to exist. C.T. Russell stated, "The *man* Jesus is
dead, forever dead."[111] The body of Jesus, whether, as they claim,
dissolved into gases or preserved as a future memorial, was not
what was raised from the dead.[112] A new creation—the "better"
Michael—was the one who appeared to the disciples by tem-
porarily materializing a human body for them to see, much as the
angels had in Genesis chapter 19.

In light of the above we may deduce several conclusions concerning the Jesus of the Watchtower Society.

Jesus never incarnated

As Nelson and Smith conclude,

> The 1921 edition of *The Harp of God* declares, "The incarnation is scripturally erroneous. Indeed, if he (Christ) had been an incarnate being, he could never have redeemed mankind" (p. 101). Witnesses teach a total *kenosis*, that is, Christ had been a spiritual being, but on coming to this world he ceased being such and became nothing more than a perfect man.[113]

Jesus of Nazareth is dead

> Today only the new Michael exists. Dr. Bjornstad observes: "When Jesus died, he was annihilated. As a human being he was simply blotted out of existence. He just ceased to exist."[114]

Jesus was not bodily resurrected

If Jesus ceased to exist, He could not have been resurrected. According to the WS, there was only an improved spiritual *re-creation* of the old Michael.[115] Thus, the new Jesus (Michael) bears no marks of the crucifixion and, therefore, could *not* have been the same person as Jesus on earth.[116] (But again, Jehovah's Witnesses speak of him as being the same person: "Regarding a future 'coming,' *Jesus himself* made it plain that at *his* second coming he would not be in the flesh, visible to humans. *He* was resurrected as a spirit.")[117] At this point, Bjornstad comments that Watchtower theology actually requires the permanent extinction of Jesus:

> If it was not the material part of Jesus that was raised, perhaps it was his immaterial nature—his soul and/or his spirit. According to the Jehovah's Witnesses, the soul and the body are the same thing. So, if his body did not rise, his soul did not rise from the dead. Furthermore, the Jehovah's Witnesses believe that the spirit is nothing more than breath. In dying

Jesus gave up this spirit or breathed his last breath, and thus his spirit could not be raised from the dead. If it was not the body of Jesus nor his soul nor his spirit that was raised from the dead, what then was resurrected according to Jehovah's Witnesses? In actuality it was nothing. It was not Jesus who rose from the dead.[118]

This is why Jehovah had to re-create Michael as a new immortal spirit, for nothing was left of Jesus of Nazareth:

Though Jehovah's Witnesses affirm belief in the resurrection of Jesus Christ, they do not really believe in his resurrection. Jehovah's Witnesses believe in re-creation. They believe that Jehovah remembers your life pattern and then creates you again, or re-creates you after death as He remembers you. In Jesus' case, Jehovah remembered the pre-human existence of Jesus as an angel, and thus re-created the angel Michael, the archangel, only this time immortal and of a divine order.[119]

The WS teaches that in the process of re-creation, Jehovah did not look to the material human stage of "Jesus" existence, but to His previous existence as an "angel."

The second coming of "Jesus" has already occurred invisibly

Jehovah's Witnesses initially taught that Christ returned in 1874; however, the date was later changed to 1914 (see Question 23). Because He was "resurrected" (re-created) as a spirit creature, His return could not possibly be in a physical body, but it had to be in a spiritual body. Thus His coming was "invisible."

According to the Watchtower Society, since the 1914 return of Jesus, He is now more important than He was prior to 1914. Why? Because for 1900 years, practically speaking, He was not a King. They claim that He obtained His kingdom in 1914 and as a result entered into an exalted status. Therefore, He was infused with a new "royal capacity such as he had not possessed when he was down here on earth in the first century....[He was now] a personage who had greater rank, authority and power than the one [before]....This made service to him much more important now. It was a higher honor now to be in his service."[120]

In conclusion, the WS doctrine of Jesus Christ logically denies His incarnation, deity, immutability, sovereignty, eternity, birth as the Messiah, bodily resurrection, kingdom prior to 1914, physical return, and even His very existence! Yet in their door-to-door witnessing, Jehovah's Witnesses have told tens of millions of people, "We believe in the biblical Jesus Christ as our Lord and Savior!"

10

WHAT DO JEHOVAH'S WITNESSES TEACH ABOUT THE HOLY SPIRIT?

Jehovah's Witnesses teach that the Holy Spirit is not a distinct person of the Godhead but Jehovah's "impersonal active force." Their teachings on this subject are given in their text *Holy Spirit—The Force Behind the Coming New Order* and elsewhere. We summarize two principal ideas here.

The Holy Spirit is a force or energy that accomplishes God's will.

> From God there goes forth an invisible active force by means of which he gets his will done. It is not a mere influence....It is a force that is operative, and it issues forth from God who is holy....He sends it forth to accomplish what is holy. So it is correctly called "holy spirit."[121]

> It is not Jehovah's "power"...."Power" is basically the ability or capacity to act or do things and it can be latent, dormant, inactively resident in someone or

something. "Force," on the other hand, more specifically describes energy projected and exerted on persons or things, and may be defined as "an influence which produces or tends to produce motion, or change of motion."[122]

The Holy Spirit is impersonal, not personal.

It was not until the fourth century C.E. that the teaching that the holy spirit was a person and part of the "Godhead" became official church dogma. Earlier Christians, sometimes called church "fathers," did not so teach....The Scriptures themselves unite to show that God's holy spirit is not a person but is God's active force by which he accomplishes his purpose and executes his will.[123]

"...this spirit is not a person at all." "No, the holy spirit is not a person and it is not part of a Trinity. The holy spirit is God's active force that he uses to accomplish his will."[124]

11

WHAT DO JEHOVAH'S WITNESSES TEACH ABOUT SALVATION IN GENERAL?

Biblically, nothing is more important in life than having a correct understanding of salvation. As Jesus Himself taught at the start of His longest recorded prayer: "Now this is eternal life: that they may know you, the only true God, and Jesus Christ, whom you have sent" (John 17:3). Eternal life comes through a personal relationship with the one true God and His only Son, Jesus Christ (John 3:16; 5:24; 6:47).

Jehovah's Witnesses claim that they offer people the true way of salvation. The issue under consideration is whether such claims are valid and how one can know. Christians have always believed that a proper understanding of God and His will for mankind can be determined by *anyone* through an objective interpretation of the Bible. The Jehovah's Witnesses, however, believe that they *alone* constitute God's channel for disseminating divine truth. This truth is determined solely by the Governing Body, the Watchtower Society, through its own unique interpretation of the Bible, and then it is dispersed to the rest of the world by loyal believers through door-to-door witnessing, Bible studies, literature distribution, and so on.

Salvation for the individual Jehovah's Witness begins with his entrance into the Watchtower organization and subsequent obedience to that organization. In other words, only those who are Jehovah's Witnesses in good standing with the Watchtower Society can be saved, at least in this life. In speaking of the requirements of salvation we are told, "A third requirement is that we be associated with God's channel, his organization....To receive everlasting life in the [coming] earthly paradise, we must identify that organization and serve God as part of it."[125]

There are three disparate classes of individuals who are "resurrected" (re-created) and potential heirs of salvation: 1) the 144,000 elect of God, 2) the Jehovah's Witnesses "earthly class" (all other Jehovah's Witnesses), and 3) the rest of mankind. We will discuss these in more detail in a moment. Here it is important to note that there are three different salvation teachings for each of these groups of people. (A fourth class of individuals, the unsaved, obviously receive no form of salvation at all. Since Jehovah's Witnesses reject the doctrine of eternal punishment, they teach these individuals are, or will be, forever annihilated.)

The first two classes of people mentioned above (the 144,000 and all other Jehovah's Witnesses) are, by definition, members of the Watchtower Society. The third class, the rest of mankind (at least most of them), have the opportunity to earn salvation after death in their resurrection upon paradise earth. We will now discuss these three groups in a bit more detail before proceeding with our general analysis of the Watchtower doctrine of salvation.

The minority 144,000

These individuals are called "anointed" and are allegedly chosen sovereignly by God. They are said to be saved on the basis of *faith* in Jesus' ransom sacrifice. However, they must earn and maintain their own salvation, and it is on this basis that they are "elected." God provides these individuals with at least five benefits that He does not give to the two other classes of "saved" people:

1. They are now *presently* "justified" by God as long as they maintain their justified status by good works and personal righteousness.

2. They are now consecrated and anointed as priests.

3. They are specially sanctified for Jehovah's purposes.

4. They will be regenerated or born again at death just like Jesus, if they remain faithful.

5. They will then rule in heaven with God and Jesus.

The Witnesses believe that at the "resurrection," the 144,000 will be changed into spirit creatures, just as they believe Jesus was at His "resurrection." This constitutes being "born again." Thus, just like the Watchtower Jesus, they will live in heaven as spirits and not on earth as physical persons. They are thus said to be given *immortality* as spirits in heaven, in contrast to a physical *eternal life* on earth.

The majority earthly class

This class includes the vast majority of Jehovah's Witnesses—well over 99.99 percent. They are called the "other sheep" or the "great crowd." These must earn salvation while on earth, but they must somehow do so without the five benefits provided above for the 144,000. From a Christian perspective, the difficulty here is obvious. Jehovah's Witnesses reserve the new birth only for the 144,000 and this only at death. The *average* Jehovah's Witness, then, has no desire or need for spiritual rebirth, or being "born again," in this life; he or she believes that the "new birth" has relevance only for the 144,000. The average Witness sincerely believes he or she *cannot* be born again. Biblically, of course, the new birth is equivalent to salvation, and to be without the new birth is to be without salvation, as Jesus made clear in John 3:3-5. In effect, to its dishonor, the Watchtower Society has denied biblical salvation to the average member, who believes he or she must earn salvation without being born again. They are then taught that *if* they are successful in earning their salvation they will be given positions of leadership in the millennial age. However, they are also warned that if they do not pass *additional* severe millennial tests, they will forfeit their eternal life and be annihilated.

Unfortunately, Witnesses who sincerely believe they are living for God and pleasing Him do not have the salvation freely offered in the Bible. Because of WS teaching, they have no desire to be born again. Thus, all their natural efforts are, as far as God is concerned, profitless for salvation, which is by grace alone, through faith alone, leading to genuine spiritual rebirth. In effect, Jehovah's Witnesses teach that *unsaved* men and women can please God entirely in their own power apart from regeneration. Nothing could be more impossible (Ephesians 2:1-10).[126]

The rest of mankind

The WS teaches that these are resurrected to life on earth in the exact moral condition in which they died (good or evil), and they must then seek to attain their own perfection during the millennium. *If* they attain perfection *and* also pass the final millennial test by avoiding the judgment of God described in Revelation 20:7-9, they will obtain eternal life on earth, which, being earthly, is distinguished from the immortality of the spiritually re-created 144,000.

12

WHAT DO JEHOVAH'S WITNESSES TEACH ABOUT SALVATION BY WORKS?

As we will emphasize while answering this question, Jehovah's Witnesses stress works-salvation, something the Bible condemns in the clearest terms (Galatians chapters 2–3; Ephesians 2:8-9). This emphasis on salvation by works is frankly admitted in Watchtower publications.

In *Man's Salvation Out of World Distress at Hand!* a chapter is titled "Requirements for Entering Spiritual Paradise." Here it is asserted: "Ways and thoughts approved by the God of righteousness are a requirement for gaining entrance to the spiritual paradise of His worshipers and servants."[127] "For persons who listen to and obey God's commandments it can mean an eternal future."[128] The "doctrinal" text *Make Sure of All Things* contains the following subheadings, quoted verbatim:

> For one to be declared righteous, he must exercise faith in the shed blood of Christ and conduct himself in harmony with that faith.[129]

> Following the Test at the End of Christ's Thousand-Year Reign, Obedient Ones Will Have Their Names Written in the Book of Life as Justified.[130]

> Knowledge of God's Word [WS doctrines] Necessary to Gain Salvation.[131 (cf. 132)]

In *Aid to Bible Understanding* (the Watchtower's biblical and theological dictionary) we find the following: "There is no substitute for obedience, no gaining of God's favor without it."[133] The *Watchtower* magazine also contains numerous examples indicating that *faith alone* is insufficient for salvation:[134-135]

> Persons desiring divine approval and eternal life must understand God's Word, declare it to others and live according to the Bible.[136]

After following through on what Jehovah God requires, the baptized disciple comes into possession of a good conscience. As long as he maintains that good conscience he is in a saved condition. Divine condemnatory judgment will not be expressed against him.[137]

The emphasis on works-salvation is true even for the 144,000, who are said to be elected by Jehovah and saved by grace. Dr. Anthony Hoekema, author of *The Four Major Cults,* points out that even after their repentance, baptism, and willingness to sacrifice all their rights on earth for the *hope* of heavenly life, even though they are allegedly "justified" (that is, have the *hope* of final justification after death), they are still not immortal and must yet earn their immortality. Only if they maintain their integrity until death will they have the opportunity for immortality, to be among the 144,000. Thus their "election" by God is on the basis of personal merit:

Jehovah's Witnesses teach that the selection of the 144,000 is a sovereign act on God's part. This selection, however, is made on the basis of their having met the requirements for membership in this class. One is chosen to belong to this group, therefore, on the basis of his worthiness. We must remember, too, that the first steps in the process that leads to salvation for this class are faith, repentance and dedication to Christ—steps that these individuals themselves must take. It is only after they have taken these steps that God justifies, regenerates, and sanctifies them. It should further be noted that much emphasis is laid on continued faithfulness to God.[138]

Hoekema thus refutes the Witnesses' claim that they believe in salvation by grace:

Hence, though Jehovah's Witnesses claim that salvation is of grace, and that all credit for salvation belongs to Jehovah, we conclude that in Watchtower theology

it is not really God's sovereign grace that saves even
the 144,000, but rather man who saves himself by
grasping the ransom, by showing himself worthy of
being selected as a member of the anointed class, and
by carrying out his dedication to Jehovah faithfully
until death.[139]

And yet, as Hoekema also observes, the remaining vast
majority of Witnesses are expected to believe that they can also
earn their own salvation without any of the declared advantages
of the 144,000:

According to Watchtower teaching, most of those
who are to be saved will attain this salvation without
being regenerated, justified (in the Christian sense),
anointed to office, and sanctified (in the Christian
sense). This means that, without having their sinful
natures renewed, this "great crowd" will be able to
have faith in Christ, to dedicate their lives wholly to
him, and to remain faithful to the end![140]

13

DOES THE BIBLE TEACH SALVATION BY GOOD WORKS?

The WS asks us to accept that Jehovah's Witnesses and the rest
of humanity will be able to save themselves by their good works
and personal righteousness. However, if anything in this life is to
be considered impossible, it must be this. The very reason Christ
died for us was because we were helpless to save ourselves. "You see,
at just the right time, *when we were still powerless*, Christ died for the
ungodly" (Romans 5:6). Indeed, to argue that we can save ourselves
is to repudiate the atonement, "for if righteousness could be gained
through the law, Christ died for nothing!" (Galatians 2:21). The
Bible is clear on this. First, no person can be saved apart from the
divine miracle of regeneration that enlivens the spirit, changes

one's disposition toward the things of God, and imparts eternal life (John 3:3-5; 6:47; 1 Corinthians 2:14-15; 2 Corinthians 5:16-17). This the Jehovah's Witnesses forbid to everyone but the 144,000, and even these are believed to receive spiritual rebirth only *after* death.

Second, no one can be saved apart from final justification in *this* life, which occurs at the point of salvation and legally declares one eternally righteous before God (Romans 3:21-31; Philippians 3:3-9). In WS doctrine, this is prohibited for the "other sheep" and for the rest of mankind. Third, no one can find acceptance with God apart from having their sins forgiven—fully and totally—something the Witnesses claim the "ransom" of Christ, by itself, did not effect (compare Revelation 21:27). Fourth, no person can live for God and please Him apart from the empowerment of the Holy Spirit, whom Witnesses believe does not exist. Clearly, the Watchtower doctrine of salvation is anything but biblical.

The Bible denies Jehovah's Witnesses doctrines when it teaches (emphasis added):

> That salvation is by grace through faith, *not* through works. "For it is by grace you have been saved, through faith—and this *not from yourselves,* it is the gift of God—not *by works,* so that no one can boast" (Ephesians 2:8-9).

> That *complete* forgiveness of *all* sins occurred at Calvary. "In him [Jesus] we *have* redemption through his blood, the forgiveness of sins" and, "He forgave us *all* our sins" (Ephesians 1:7; Colossians 2:13).

> That full and entire justification occurs in *this* life at the *moment* of faith. "Therefore, since we *have been justified* through faith, we *have peace* with God through our Lord Jesus Christ.…Since we have *now been justified* by his blood, *how much more* shall we be saved from God's wrath through him!" (Romans 5:1,9).

That eternal life is a *present* possession of all true believers. "I tell you the truth, he who believes *has everlasting life*" (John 6:47).

The truth is that Christ atoned for *all* our sins on the cross, not just the sins of Adam or potentially the sins of most. This is why salvation is entirely by grace and why God does not expect us to earn our salvation by good works, or to achieve the potential forgiveness of our sins by obedience. Christ earned full salvation for us so that we only need receive it as a gift.

The Bible clearly teaches that salvation is a free gift. By definition, a free gift cannot be paid for. The *Oxford American Dictionary* defines gift as "a thing given or received without payment." No man takes a gift of flowers home to his wife and says, "Hi, honey, these are yours when you wash the car." In the same way, no one pays for salvation with his or her works when it has been freely given as a gift. Biblically, "the *gift* of God is eternal life" (Romans 6:23); and we are "justified *freely* by his grace" (Romans 3:24), because we have "the *gift* of righteousness" (Romans 5:17). The Witness concept of salvation, then, disavows the biblical teaching on salvation by grace through faith alone (Romans 3:28):

> William J. Schnell points out that during his years with the movement the other sheep were told that if they stayed close to the Watchtower organization, listened attentively to its indoctrination, went out regularly to distribute literature, and rigidly reported the time spent in doing so, they might be saved at Armageddon! All the emphasis, he insists, was on works, particularly on witnessing, as the way to arrive at a reasonable certainty of future salvation, rather than on faith in Jesus Christ as Saviour.[141]

Here is the crux of the problem: Witnesses do not teach that salvation comes by faith in Jesus but, in essence, by faith in what the Watchtower Society tells them to believe and do.

14

HAVE THE JEHOVAH'S WITNESSES MADE THE BIBLICAL DOCTRINE OF SALVATION IRRELEVANT TO EVERYONE?

William Schnell also points out another major consequence of the Witness view of salvation. It nullifies the relevance of most New Testament texts related to salvation for the vast majority of Jehovah's Witnesses (and everyone else). Why? Because only the 144,000 are declared to be regenerated, chosen, justified, saints, part of the body of Christ, sanctified, heaven-bound, and so on. Therefore, all the biblical passages that speak of these and related things do *not* apply, according to WS doctrine, to the average Jehovah's Witness. It's not just that they cannot be born again, it's that most of the biblical doctrines *related* to regeneration are denied them as well.

Thus, according to WS teaching, what the Bible teaches about salvation is really applicable to only a handful of people. In effect, as far as salvation is concerned, the Bible is simply irrelevant for 99.999999 percent of humanity.[142-143]

In 1980 it was reported that a number of high-ranking Jehovah's Witnesses at Bethel headquarters were disfellowshipped or voluntarily left the Watchtower Society. It seems that their personal Bible studies had caused them to believe—quite correctly—that everyone, not just the 144,000, needed to be born again. Among this new crop of outcasts were Raymond Franz, nephew of former president F.W. Franz, and Edward Dunlap, former 12-year head of the Watchtower Society Gilead School of the Bible, its missionary training arm.[144] But, as is so often the case with authoritarian religions, the Watchtower Society would not tolerate dissent; appropriate action was taken to silence the "heresy."

Indeed, the personal fear that individual members may be subject to is not small—for example, under threat of eternal annihilation, believers must seek to maintain their own personal righteousness under virtually impossible circumstances, perhaps explaining, in part, why there are so many dropouts and such a high rate of mental illness among the Witnesses.[145-59]

Unfortunately, in the logic of WS doctrine, no Jehovah's Witnesses anywhere can have any assurance of their salvation. Former Jehovah's Witnesses themselves have pointed out the uncertain and tenuous nature of their status before God. "I never had any assurance of my salvation; it was something to be obtained by right conduct and good works as a theocratic slave. In spite of all my efforts I did not have a personal relationship with the Lord Jesus Christ. If a Witness does not maintain a faithful course of integrity, he loses his chance of gaining everlasting life....This teaching applied even to the 'heavenly class' of 144,000." (Cited in Edmond Gruss, *We Left Jehovah's Witnesses,* p. 132.)

The WS denies all of this. Like Mormons, Jehovah's Witnesses may stress that they do not teach salvation on the basis of works of righteousness. They do this by maintaining an arbitrary distinction between Mosaic works, which cannot save, and New Testament works, which can save. The goal is to attempt to reconcile their doctrine of works-salvation with biblical statements denying works-salvation. Whenever the Bible denies works-salvation, the WS argues it must be referring to trying to earn one's salvation by outdated Mosaic works, not required Gospel works. In effect, there are dead works of "the Law" not saving works of "the Gospel." In denying salvation by works of the Law[160] while asserting salvation by works of the Gospel,[161] Witnesses may claim to deny salvation by works, while in fact supporting it.[162]

The difficulty with the Watchtower argument is that, morally speaking, Mosaic law and Gospel law are not that easily separated. Further, the requirements of the Gospel law are considerably more stringent than the law of Moses, as passages like the Sermon on the Mount (Matthew 5–7) make clear.

15

WHAT DO JEHOVAH'S WITNESSES TEACH ABOUT THE ATONEMENT OF CHRIST?

In speaking with individual Jehovah's Witnesses, it may initially seem as if they believe in Christ's atoning death on the cross. Certainly they claim this. But the Witnesses actually oppose the biblical doctrine of the atonement, as numerous Christian scholars and researchers have recognized. The late Dr. Walter Martin called their view of the atonement "completely unscriptural."[163] Professor Edmond Gruss, a former Jehovah's Witness and author of the definitive *Apostles of Denial*, declares, "The Witnesses' view of the atonement is very different from that held by orthodoxy and in essence is a rejection of that Biblical doctrine."[164] In his book *The Four Major Cults*, Anthony Hoekema agrees.[165]

Gruss points out that during their early history the Witnesses actually had three entirely different views of the "ransom" of Christ. "The teaching of the Society on the ransom of Christ has been confused from the beginning, with C.T. Russell presenting three differing positions on this doctrine in the publications of the Watchtower Society. The teaching on the subject since Russell's death has also been unsteady as to the extent and application of the ransom."[166]

How does the Witness view of the atonement differ from the biblical view? The key difference can be seen in their *limitation* of the atonement. They believe Christ's death made *potential* forgiveness available for others by faith and works. Just as Adam's disobedience brought death, so Christ's obedience brought life—resurrection (that is, re-creation)—with the potential to earn eternal life. But Christ's death alone did not atone for everyone's sins; in the end, good works and good character do this. Thus the Christian concept of a completed atonement of infinite value is rejected.

For some people, according to WS teaching, Christ's death has no value at all because there are some sins that are simply unforgivable. Apparently, certain murderers and the willfully rebellious receive no benefit. For example, Adam is stated to be exempt from the benefits of the atonement because he was a "willful sinner."[167] "Under the law the deliberate murderer could not be ransomed. Adam, by his willful course, brought death on all mankind, hence was a murderer" (Romans 5:12 NWT). "Thus the sacrificed life of Jesus is not acceptable to God as a ransom for the sinner Adam."[168]

What the Watchtower fails to recognize is that *all* people everywhere are "willful sinners." That is the essence of being a sinner, as the Bible plainly declares (Romans 1:18–2:5; 3:9-20; Ephesians 2:1-3; Colossians 1:21). In addition, the Bible teaches that murderers can be forgiven, and there are several biblical examples of forgiven murderers, such as Moses (Exodus 2:12); King David (2 Samuel 11:14-15; 12:9) and possibly the apostle Paul (Acts 8:1; 9:1; 22:4-5; 26:10). Even to those who murdered Him, Jesus responded, "Father, forgive them" (Luke 23:34). But according to the Watchtower, there are millions of other people for whom the atonement has had no value, and they have already been annihilated forever.[169]

Even though the atonement, according to WS doctrine, involved the death of only a man (Jesus), Jehovah's Witnesses believe it could somehow be applied to more than one man. The Witnesses refer to a "corresponding ransom" theory in presenting this idea. As is true in The Way International, another Arian group, the Witnesses argue Jesus had to be *only* a man in order to be our Savior:

> If Jesus, when he was baptized at thirty years of age, had been a so-called God-man...he would have been superhuman and would have had more value than a ransom for all mankind. The perfect justice of God would not unjustly accept more value than that of the thing to be ransomed....It was the perfect man Adam that had sinned and so had lost for his offspring

human perfection and its privileges. Jesus must likewise be humanly perfect, to correspond with the sinless Adam in Eden. In that way he could offer a ransom that *exactly* corresponded in value with what the sinner Adam lost for his descendants. This requirement of divine justice did not allow for Jesus to be more than a perfect man. That is why, in writing 1 Timothy 2:5-6, the apostle Paul uses a special word in Greek, *antilutron,* to describe what Jesus offered in sacrifice to God.[170]

The human life that Jesus Christ laid down in sacrifice must be exactly equal to that life which Adam forfeited for all his offspring: it must be a perfect human life, no more, no less. It must be a "corresponding ransom."[171]

What the Witnesses miss here is that one *man* alone could never atone for the sins of *billions* of sinners. Only if Jesus were both God and man could His atonement forgive all human sin. Nevertheless, somehow, Jehovah's Witnesses apply the death of one man to all "capable" of receiving it through good works (some murderers and certain others being excluded).[172]

Hoekema correctly questions this reasoning:

For, as has been pointed out, there is no real continuity between Christ as he appeared in the flesh and [as] the previously existing Archangel Michael. For the Witnesses, therefore, God did not really send his only-begotten Son (even if one understands this term as designating the created Logos) into the world to ransom man from his sins. Rather, He caused a sinless man to be miraculously conceived by Mary; this man was not even a "spirit-begotten son of God" at birth, but only a human son. He was different from other men only in two respects: (1) he had been born of a virgin, and (2) he lived a perfect life....At this point the question cannot be suppressed: Why should the sacrificed life of Jesus Christ have so much value that

it can serve to ransom millions of people from annihilation? It was a perfect human life which was sacrificed, to be sure; we must not minimize this point.
But it was the perfect human life of someone who was
only a man. Could the life of a mere man, offered in
sacrifice, serve to purchase a multitude which no man
can number?[173]

The Scripture is clear on this: the death of one *man* is insufficient to ransom another: "No *man* can redeem the life of another
or give to God a ransom for him—the ransom for a life is costly,
no payment is ever enough" (Psalm 49:7-8, emphasis added).
Only God can redeem a life, which is precisely why Christ had to
be God and precisely why Christ died.

Further, as Gruss points out, the Greek word *antilutron* does
not carry the meaning of "exact correspondence," which the Witnesses have attributed to it:

The "corresponding ransom" doctrine should be
rejected on the following grounds: First, the Greek
word *antilutron* occurs only once in the Bible (1 Timothy 2:6) and the meaning need not be much different than *lutron* ("ransom"). After an examination
of the words in the *lutron* group in the New Testament, Morris concludes that in meaning *antilutron*
"does not seem to differ greatly from the simple
lutron, but the preposition emphasizes the thought of
substitution; it is a 'substitute-ransom' that is signi-
fied. Such a term well suits the context, for we read of
Christ 'who gave himself on behalf of all' (1 Timothy
2:6). The thought clearly resembles that of Mark
10:45, i.e., that Jesus had died in the stead of those
who deserved death. If the thought of substitution is
there, we find it here to an even greater degree in view
of the addition of the preposition which emphasizes
substitution."

It should be obvious to the reader that what the Watchtower writers convey with the words "corresponding ransom" and what is conveyed by the words "substitute ransom" as explained by Morris and the rest of the Scriptures are not remotely the same.[174]

As in Mormonism, Watchtower writings speak highly of "the atonement." But as to its importance, both the LDS and the WS relegate it to a secondary status behind human good works. It is not faith in Christ that applies the merits of Christ, but the good works and perseverance of the individual and his faith in the Watchtower Society. Without these, the merits of Christ are worthless.[175] A former Witness of 16 years points out that, despite their claims to believe in the atonement, the Witnesses deny this through their demand for works:

> As I laid aside *The Watchtower* and other study guides of the Jehovah's Witnesses and read the New Testament with an open mind, I became aware of two things. First, salvation comes by faith in Jesus Christ and not by works (Ephesians 2:8-10)....I found out that they said one thing but believed another. They will often speak highly of Jesus' sacrifice and yet deny its efficacy by saying that to be saved one must do all the things the organization directs.[176]

There is an additional sense in which the death of Christ is secondary. Jehovah's Witnesses teach that the primary goal of Jesus was to vindicate the name of Jehovah in response to a challenge of Satan's; it was only Jesus' secondary purpose to die for the consequences of Adam's sin. In other words, Jesus' principal goal was *not* to die for our sins.[177] Dr. James Bjornstad comments,

> His primary purpose was to vindicate (provide a defense for Jehovah's name) and establish Jehovah's kingdom....After Adam disobeyed God, Satan challenged God to put a creature on earth who could experience all the temptations Satan could give and still remain faithful to God until death....The burden

fell upon His first created being, His son, Michael the archangel. God's son came to earth as Jesus and met all the temptations of Satan, according to the Jehovah's Witnesses. Moreover, he remained true to God until death. In so doing he was able to establish God's kingdom. Thus Jesus was Jehovah's chief witness. Jehovah's Witnesses claim Jesus also had a secondary purpose in being here. He came to sacrifice his human body as a ransom to God for Adam's sin.[178]

Further, Jehovah's Witnesses not only deny a *completed* atonement by declaring its practical application dependent on works, but also deny it by declaring its future application occurs only at the end of the millennium. It is at "the end of Christ's thousand-year reign as King when he finishes applying the merit of his human sacrifice."[179] Dr. Martin correctly observes,

> Jehovah's Witnesses argue that the atonement is not wholly of God, despite 2 Corinthians 5:21, but rather half of God and half of man. Jesus, according to their argument, removed the effects of Adam's sin by His sacrifice on Calvary, but the work will not be fully completed until the survivors of Armageddon return to God through free will and become subject to the theocratic rule of Jehovah.[180]

In conclusion, the Jehovah's Witnesses view of salvation and the atonement of Christ must be considered deficient and powerless to save. It does not accept God's teaching about salvation, and therefore it cannot have God's blessing.

16

WHAT DO JEHOVAH'S WITNESSES TEACH ABOUT MAN AND THE AFTERLIFE?

Jehovah's Witnesses believe that man is a creation of Jehovah but deny that man is created in God's image with an immortal soul. In Watchtower theology the body *is* the soul. Man consists of a mortal body (the soul) and the mortal life energy that activates it (the spirit or breath, or "life force"). For Jehovah's Witnesses, the devil is the author of the idea of an eternal soul, as he is the author of all Christian doctrine.[181]

The soul is material and mortal, not immaterial and immortal.

> The Scriptures show that both *psykhe* and *ne'phesh,* as used with reference to earthly creatures, refer to that which is material, tangible, visible and mortal....The Scriptures clearly show that *ne'phesh* and *psykhe* are used to designate the animal creation lower than man. The same terms apply to man... So, too, the "spirit"... or life force of man is not distinct from the life force in animals....*Psykhe* does not refer to something immortal or indestructible.[182]

The spirit is not the soul.

> The "spirit" (Hebrew, *ru'ahh:* Greek, *pneu'ma*) should not be confused with the "soul" (Hebrew, *ne'phesh;* Greek, *psykhe'*), for they refer to different things....As has been shown, the soul *(ne'phesh; psykhe')* is the creature itself. The spirit *(ru'ahh; pneu'ma)* generally refers to the life force of the living creature or soul, though the original language terms may also have other meanings.[183]

If man has no immortal spirit, he cannot be subject to eternal punishment. Again, for the WS, the soul is the body and the spirit is just the breath, so when the body dies, the person is extinguished. (This explains why Jehovah's Witnesses actually believe in re-creation, not resurrection.) As a result, Jehovah's Witnesses deny the biblical teaching of death as separation from God; they prefer a materialistic interpretation of total annihilation or extinction. The doctrine of hell is believed to be a satanic teaching. Annihilation is God's only judgment or "punishment" on sin.

There is no hell.

> The teaching about a fiery hell...can rightly be designated as a "teaching of demons."...Has not this doctrine...grossly misrepresented God?...Those teaching the hellfire doctrine are therefore saying blasphemous things against God....That being the case, would you want to continue supporting any religious system that teaches a fiery hell?[184]

Death is extinction.

> Biblical evidence thus makes it plain that those whom God judges as undeserving of life will experience, not eternal torment in a literal fire, but "everlasting destruction." They will not be preserved alive anywhere. The fire of Gehenna is therefore not a symbol of the totality and thoroughness of that destruction.[185]

Heaven is only for the elect (144,000).

As we have seen, the vast majority of Jehovah's Witnesses and re-created mankind inherit an earthly paradise; only the 144,000 go to heaven. The subheadings in *Make Sure of All Things* declare: "Only a limited number from among mankind to be in heaven with the Lamb Jesus Christ....144,000 are spiritual Israelites, include both Jews and Gentiles....Chosen by God for heavenly life....Other faithful servants of God to be rewarded with life on earth, not in heaven."[186]

Summary

In the end, the WS teaches that there are three basic possibilities for the future state after death:

1. Re-creation as a spirit in heaven (immortality as one of the 144,000 elect).

2. Re-creation to a probationary general future physical life on earth for a thousand years.

3. Depending upon the outcome of this life and its various testings, there will result either eternal life upon earth or eternal extinction.

17

DOES THE WATCHTOWER SOCIETY SUPPORT THE OCCULT?

"This is not what some may regard as spiritism by any means...."

—Judge Rutherford describing his angelic
inspiration (*Light,* Book 1, 1930, p. 64.)

Jehovah's Witnesses claim to oppose all occult practices. However, the WS has been involved in occult activity historically, so denials today should be accepted with a grain of salt. Indeed, this appears to be largely a matter of semantics. For example, when it comes to accepting spiritistic inspiration, they have simply redefined this as inspiration from "angels" or "holy spirit."

The Bible Way Productions, Inc. (a Watchtower sect started by Roy D. Goodrich of Ft. Lauderdale, FL), published a 36-page pamphlet (1969 ed.), No. 272, "Demonism and the Watchtower," which gives evidence that during significant portions of the Rutherford era the Society apparently engaged in work with spiritistically associated radionic devices such as the Abrams' "blackbox." (Abrams, like practitioners of occult radionics and psychometry generally, was involved with spiritism.) Although the "devices" are held to be the source of psychic power (for example, healing energy), it is invariably the spirit behind the device which is the real source of power, as we documented elsewhere.[187] In light of this involvement, Goodrich raises a significant question: "Since the 'Diagnostic Machine of Dr. Albert Abrams' at Jonesboro, Ark., and the 'Radioclast,' its present counterpart so long housed and used at the Bethel home, are both ideal for receiving 'yes' and 'no' answers from the occult realm, have we any assurance that these have not been so used in the formulation of Watch Tower doctrines, policies and commandments?"[188]

As we will see, they were so used. Also, Russell's and the Society's endorsement of numerological-prophetic power to the Great Pyramid of Egypt seems to have had occult associations.[189] Thus it can be documented that the Watchtower Society in its early years was involved in the occult.[190] Even though the Society's official position toward occult activity historically is supposedly in agreement with the prohibition found in Deuteronomy 18:9-12, that this is not the case can be seen from the work of additional researchers. For example, the Watchtower Information Service (www.watchtowerinformationservice.org) provides articles on WS use of astrology and other divination, necromancy and other spiritism, Egyptian religion, and more. The first six or seven issues of Ken Raines' *JW Research Journal* also have the Watchtower Society and the occult as a principal theme. At Raines' website, one can find a dozen articles like the following: "The Spirit World Guided Rutherford"; "Was Rutherford a Spirit Medium?" and "Talking with the Dead: JWs and Necromancy" (www.premier1.net/~raines/articles.html).

Today the Watchtower Society appears to be unsuspectingly involved in the occult in principally one manner: It seems to accept demonic guidance and revelations that come to it in the guise of angelic contacts. Nor is this something new. For example, Judge Rutherford practiced what a channeler or medium would practice when wanting to contact the spirit world. But Rutherford defined his practice differently, as godly contact with angels. This, too, is what countless channelers today would argue. However, no godly angel is going to supply revelations that deny God, Christ, and salvation as the Bible teaches them.

Because the Watchtower's translation, doctrines, and practices have failed to meet biblical, scholarly, and sometimes moral[191] standards, how could supernatural assistance they claim to receive have originated in God? Would godly angels lend help to an organization that denies the true nature of God, deliberately distorts His Word, and rejects His Son? The Bible says that fallen angels—demons—would do this. The Bible further declares that demons masquerade as "angels of light" while doing this (2 Corinthians 11:14-15).

The Watchtower Society claims that "angels" actually guided its leaders in translating the *New World Translation* of the Bible, but Bill Cetnar, a former service department member in the Jehovah's Witnesses headquarters at Brooklyn, New York, found that many Watchtower beliefs were also professed by Johannes Greber, a spirit-possessed medium the Society was quoting.[192]

Let's look at some examples of the Society's claims to supernatural guidance. Judge Rutherford openly stated that angels helped write the *Watchtower* magazine when he said that "the Lord through His angel sees to it that the information is given to His people in due time...." and, "Angels deliver what is published."[193] Ken Raines points out that Rutherford claimed that Jehovah God was the actual editor of the *Watchtower* magazine, and that "angels transmitted the divine interpretation of Scripture into his mind." Further, "most of the unique doctrines and chronology that JWs believe today came from angels via Rutherford's angelic channeling." (Ken Raines, "Rutherford and Biblical Interpretation: Angelic Channeling, Part 1," *JW Research*, Vol. 1, no. 1, Winter, 1994, p. 2.) Rutherford also endorsed a book called *Angels and Women* (1924), which was received through the occult method of automatic writing, admittedly "by one of the fallen angels who desired to come back into divine favor" (p. 5). Allegedly, Rutherford endorsed this book because he truly believed that some demons were honest and could still be saved from annihilation. So we see numerous WS claims that the *Watchtower* was inspired by angels or holy spirit. "The *Watchtower* is not the instrument of any man or set of men....No man's opinion is expressed in The *Watchtower*." ("Taught of God," the *Watchtower*, November 1, 1931.)

Former worldwide president of Jehovah's Witnesses F.W. Franz also spoke of angels guiding the Watchtower: "We believe that the angels of God are used in directing Jehovah's Witnesses."[194]

Among other things, the *Watchtower* claims that angels 1) enlighten and comfort, 2) bring refreshing truths, and 3) transmit information to "God's anointed people."[195] In another clear statement, the *Watchtower* magazine admits, "Jehovah's Witnesses today make their declaration of the good news of the kingdom under angelic direction and support."[196]

In the *Watchtower*, December 1, 1981 (p. 27) and July 15, 1960 (p. 439), the leaders of the Jehovah's Witnesses claim to be God's "channel of communication," actively "channeling" (the early use of this common New Age term is theirs) since the days of Rutherford. In the issue of April 1, 1972 (p. 200), they claim that all spiritual direction is supplied by invisible angels. In the issues of November 15, 1933 (p. 344), November 1, 1935 (p. 331) and December 15, 1987 (p. 7), they claim that the name "Jehovah's Witnesses" and their key doctrine of "Christ's" invisible return in 1914 were channeled by invisible angels. Today the Society's leaders claim that both "holy spirit" and "angels" communicate information to them (the *Watchtower*, March 1, 1972, p. 155; August 1, 1987, p. 19).[197] "Angels may share in directing us, or we may receive guidance by holy spirit" (the *Watchtower*, July 15, 1992, p. 21).

The official WS website carries the following statement:

> This scripture [Revelation 14:6-7] highlights the foremost work of the angels today. They are involved in a high-priority assignment—that of declaring the good news of God's Kingdom. It was with regard to this work that Jesus promised his followers: "I am with

you all the days until the conclusion of the system of things." (Matthew 28:18-20) How is Jesus with his followers? One way is by providing them with angelic help so that this monumental work might be accomplished....Angelic guidance, along with the Witnesses' own initiative, has resulted in hundreds of thousands coming to a knowledge of Jehovah each year! (www.watchtower.org/library/w/1995/11/1/the _truth_about_angels.htm from the *Watchtower,* November 1, 1995.)

Indeed, few would deny that it was under second president Rutherford's "angelic guidance" that the Witnesses received most of their basic doctrines of today. Rutherford believed that God's "holy spirit" had ceased to function as his teacher and had been replaced by angels who taught him in his mind (the *Watchtower,* September 1, 1930, p. 263; February 1, 1935, p. 41; Rutherford, *Riches* [1936], p. 316).

Direct "angelic" guidance was also the source behind the WS *New World Translation.* According to the Scottish *Daily Express,* F.W. Franz testified:

1. That he and N.H. Knorr headed the secret Translation Committee of seven.

2. That he and Knorr, not the Committee, had the last word.

3. That he, Franz, was the head of the Society's Publicity Department.

4. That translations and interpretations emanated from God in this way:

   a. They are INVISIBLY COMMUNICATED to the Publicity Department.

   b. This is accomplished by "ANGELS OF DIFFERENT RANKS WHO CONTROL WITNESSES."[198]

This statement, cited by Professor Gruss, was checked by him for accuracy, and is also quoted by Goodrich as accurate.[199] Alleged "angels...who control witnesses" sounds more like angels of the less-than-friendly type. If the Watchtower Society leadership truly was "possessed by angels," it seems evident that they were not of the kind that ministered to Jesus.

In truth, in the last century, the WS has flipped back and forth concerning both its acceptance and interpretation of occult phenomena. For example, "However, in a complete flip-flop the WTS in 1989 reverted back to their necromantic belief: 'It is fitting, then, that one of the 24 elders, representing anointed ones already in heaven, should stir John's thinking...(Revelation 7:13-14a). Yes, that elder could locate the answer and give it to John. This suggests that resurrected ones of the 24-elders group may be involved in the communicating of divine truths today.'"[200]

It would appear, then, that the WS has been consistently involved in the occult throughout its history, albeit characteristically under another name. Since it continues to claim to receive supernatural revelation as to biblical interpretation, prophecy, and teaching from angels, "holy spirit," and "heavenly elders," the Jehovah's Witnesses should be classed as an occult religion despite its denials.

A CRITIQUE OF THE WATCHTOWER SOCIETY AND JEHOVAH'S WITNESSES

In this section we will concentrate on documenting one basic point: the inherent untrustworthiness of the Watchtower Society.[201] Although we do touch on other areas, we emphasize this one because of its importance. If a Jehovah's Witness finds that he cannot trust the Watchtower Society as the sole channel of God on earth, it will be difficult for him to remain a Witness. As we saw earlier, many do have doubts. Either the Watchtower Society *is* God's sole channel, and as such should be, at least generally, biblically accurate, morally upright, and generally trustworthy, or it *is not* God's channel. If it is an organization propagating the conflicting beliefs and theories of men, or perhaps so-called "angels," who are not receiving direction and guidance from God, it is better avoided. As we quoted Judge Rutherford earlier, "It is entirely unsafe for the people to rely upon the words and doctrines of imperfect men"—let alone imperfect "angels."

The following information will adequately answer the question, "Is the Watchtower Society God's true channel for giving truth to the world or is it a fallible organization beset with sufficient corruption to thoroughly dispel its claims to divine guidance?" We think the latter, and many open-minded former Witnesses will agree. [202] An Internet blurb on Randall Waters' *Thus Saith the Governing Body of Jehovah's Witnesses* noted the WS "has made more changes in doctrine, more coverups and has promoted more outright deceptions than most religions put together." The question must be asked: If truth is what we should expect from men directly guided by God for over 100 years, how is it we get the opposite in the Watchtower Society?

We have selected four principal "tests":

1. Does the WS uphold honesty and integrity in translating the Bible, God's Word?

2. Is the WS trustworthy and accurate in its prophetic statements?

3. Has the WS changed its own divine revelations?

4. Is the WS fair and accurate in quoting other sources and authors in support of its views?

18

CAN THE WATCHTOWER SOCIETY'S *NEW WORLD TRANSLATION* BE TRUSTED?

Our first test will be to examine the Watchtower translation, *The New World Translation of the Holy Scriptures* (NWT). As we will note, both their English Bible and their Greek Interlinear claim great fidelity to the original languages and absolute accuracy in translation. However, if the Witnesses have not translated God's revelation with care and accuracy, but have incorporated their own doctrinal bias in complete disregard of the Greek text, then it is unlikely that the Watchtower Bible and Tract Society (WBTS) is God's sole channel for communicating His will to mankind today. Indeed, the combined weight of the following indisputable facts proves that the Watchtower Society has little regard at all for the Word of God. These three facts are: 1) pervasive unbiblical theology, 2) clear bias in translating the Bible (numerous false translations also prove that divine angels were never involved in the NWT), and 3) numerous false prophecies historically.[203]

The Emphatic Diaglott

Before we begin our analysis of the NWT, we should note that for about 70 years it was preceded in use by the *Emphatic Diaglott*, published in 1864 by Benjamin Wilson and based on the 1806 recension of J.J. Griesbach. In utilizing this translation, the Witnesses never informed their members that the translation was flawed and that Wilson was a Christadelphian, who, holding similar doctrines with Jehovah's Witnesses, naturally sought a translation in harmony with Christadelphian bias. For example, the *Diaglott* (like the NWT) translates Matthew 25:46 "agelasting cutting-off" and John 1:1 "the Word was a god," both in harmony with Christadelphian (and Watchtower) denials of eternal punishment and Christ's deity respectively.[204] Professor Emeritus Edmond Gruss, of the Master's College in Southern California, observes how the *Diaglott* fit the needs of the newly formed Russellite religion:

> Wilson was self-educated; his work shows that he certainly was not a scholar. Neither did he have the respect of those who were scholars. Obviously, his purpose was not to translate, but to justify his theological views....It may be concluded, then, that the *Emphatic Diaglott* was adopted because of its Christadelphian bias which agreed almost perfectly with the new Russellite group that was forming. The Russellites accepted the renderings of Wilson, for they did not have the linguistic ability either to evaluate or to determine their correctness, nor did they wish to question that which so perfectly supported their theories....[205]

In spite of his bias and errors in translation, Wilson claimed "scrupulous fidelity" to the original languages. "Scrupulous fidelity has been maintained throughout this version in giving the true rendering of the original text into English; no regard whatever being paid to the prevailing doctrines or prejudices of sects, or the peculiar tenets of theologians. To the Divine authority of the original Scriptures alone has there been the most humble and unbiased submission."[206]

As we will see, the Jehovah's Witnesses make similar claims to scholarly objectivity in Bible translations and yet fail miserably to live up to them.

The New World Translation (NWT) of the Holy Scriptures

> Another mark of true religion is that its members have a *deep respect for the Bible.* They accept it as the Word of God and believe what it says.[207]

After using the *Diaglott* for many years, eventually the Watchtower Society produced its own translation, *The New World Translation of the Holy Scriptures* (NWT). As noted, testimony under oath by then vice president F.W. Franz revealed that translations and interpretations came from God in such a way that they were invisibly communicated to the publicity department via "angels of various ranks who control witnesses."[208] Indeed, two mediumistic translations that claim to originate in the spirit world have translations similar to those of the NWT. For example, the 1937 New Testament translation by spiritistic medium Johannes Greber has similar translations for John 1:1, Hebrews 1:8, and other verses and is quoted by the WBTS in several of its books.[209] Spirit possession would indeed explain the theological bias and anti-Christian nature of the Society's translation.

Dr. Robert M. Bowman Jr. points out that readers should not assume that the NWT only has a relatively small number of errors in its translation relative to key doctrines, and that, for the most part, the NWT is an acceptable translation. The truth is that there are hundreds and thousands of distortions of the Bible in the NWT. "The JWs *systematically* distort the Bible to make it fit their preconceived beliefs....The NWT itself reflects this systematic distortion in a vast number of texts relating to practically every area of biblical doctrine."[210] Even a small listing of WS mistranslations, in addition to those listed later, include: Genesis 1:2; Exodus 3:14; Numbers 1:52; Ecclesiastes 12:7; Isaiah 43:10; Matthew 2:11; Mark 1:4; Luke 23:43; John 6:56; 14:17; Acts 2:42; 10:36; Romans 2:29; 8:1; 1 Corinthians 6:19; 10:4; Philippians 1:23; 2:9; Colossians 1:19; 1 Timothy 4:1; Hebrews 12:9; 12:23; 1 John 5:20. (Many of these scriptural mistranslations will not seem significant unless one understands Watchtower theology. Securing a book such as Bowman's *Jehovah's Witnesses Answered Verse by Verse* will be a good reference for those readers wishing to pursue the matter.)

Nevertheless, the Watchtower Society has made many statements concerning NWT translation accuracy. Of course, if Witnesses really believed the translators were possessed by "angels," it would be easy to assume the translation was accurate even when the translators themselves did not know the original languages. Regardless, we find the WBTS claiming absolute fidelity to the Greek and Hebrew text. Their *Kingdom Interlinear Translation of the Greek Scriptures* declares: "Its literal interlinear English translation is specially designed to open up to the student of the Sacred Scriptures what the original Koine Greek basically or literally says, without any sectarian religious coloration."[211] And of the NWT, the Society asserts:

> The translators who have a fear and love of the divine Author of the Holy Scriptures feel especially a responsibility toward Him to transmit his thoughts and declarations as accurately as possible. They also feel a responsibility toward the searching readers of the modern translation who depend upon the inspired Word of the Most High God for their everlasting salvation. It was with such a sense of solemn responsibility that the committee of dedicated men have produced the New World Translation of the Holy Scriptures, over the course of many years.[212]

In its text *All Scripture Is Inspired of God and Beneficial,* the Society makes similar claims. Note for example the assertion to grammatical accuracy:

> The New World Translation…conveys accurately the action or state expressed in the Hebrew and Greek verbs.…The conveying of the state of the Hebrew verb accurately into English is most important, otherwise the meaning may be distorted.…Similar care has been exercised in the translating of the Greek verbs.…The New World Translation…is accurate and reliable…a faithful translation of God's Word.[213]

We will later document comments on the NWT by those familiar with the original languages who have made a study of the Jehovah's Witnesses a scholarly pursuit, or are Greek scholars themselves. Then we will document the accuracy of NWT claims by citing specific examples of mistranslation from the NWT.

19

What Do Respected Scholars Say About the New World Translation?

Numerous Greek and Biblical scholars have declared that the NWT is a poor and biased translation.

Dr. Robert Countess' published doctoral dissertation, *The Jehovah's Witness New Testament: A Critical Analysis of the New World Translation of the Christian Greek Scriptures* (Phillipsburg, NJ: Presbyterian and Reformed Publications, 1982), offers a most thorough and devastating critique of the NWT. His overall conclusion is that the NWT

> …has been sharply unsuccessful in keeping doctrinal considerations from influencing the actual translation…[The] New World Translation of the Christian Greek Scriptures must be viewed as a radically biased

piece of work. At some points it is actually dishonest. At others it is neither modern or scholarly. And interwoven throughout its fabric is inconsistent application of its own principles enunciated in the Foreword and Appendix.[214]

Professor Edmond Gruss, author of a standard historical and theological work, *Apostles of Denial*, writes:

A sound interpretation of any passage requires a careful grammatical exegesis. Watchtower publications repeatedly present doctrines and interpretations of the Scriptures which completely misunderstand or ignore grammar. Before the Society entered into the field of translation, there were many verses which gave them trouble because of their direct contradiction of the Witnesses' doctrines. With the appearance of the New World Translation the difficult passages in many cases were weakened or eliminated by a translation that violated or ignored the rules of grammar.[215]

Dr. Anthony Hoekema, author of *The Four Major Cults*, points out: "...the Jehovah's Witnesses actually impose their own theological system upon Scripture and force it to comply with their beliefs....[Their] New World Translation of the Bible is by no means an objective rendering of the sacred text into modern English, but is a biased translation in which many of their peculiar teachings of the Watchtower Society are smuggled into the text of the Bible itself."[216]

The late Dr. Walter Martin, author of *Jehovah of the Watchtower*, observed that of the anonymous seven-member translation committee at least five had no training in Greek:

These books possess a veneer of scholarship unrivaled for its daring and boldness in a field that all informed scholars know Jehovah's Witnesses are almost totally unprepared to venture into. As a matter of fact, the authors have been able to uncover partially a carefully guarded Watchtower secret: the names of five of the members of the New World Translation committee. Not one of these five people has any training in Greek...[or Hebrew].[217]

Dr. Bruce Metzger, professor emeritus of New Testament Language and Literature at Princeton Theological Seminary and author of *The Text of the New Testament,* states: "...the Jehovah's Witnesses have incorporated in their translation of the New Testament several quite erroneous renderings of the Greek."[218]

Dr. Julius Mantey was one of the leading Greek scholars in the world and coauthor of *The Dana-Mantey Greek Grammar* and *A Hellenistic Greek Reader.* He stated,

> I have never read any New Testament so badly translated as *The Kingdom Interlinear Translation of the Greek Scriptures.* In fact, it is not their translation at all. Rather, it is a distortion of the New Testament. The translators used what J.B. Rotherham had translated in 1893, in modern speech, and changed the readings in scores of passages to state what Jehovah's Witnesses believe and teach. That is distortion, not translation.[219] (See the Appendix for one of his letters to the WS.)

In light of the previous testimony, it must be concluded that the NWT cannot be trusted to accurately convey God's Word because of its biases in translation and lack of scholarship in many areas. Nor can Jehovah's Witnesses appeal to an alleged "trinitarian bias" on the part of these scholars, for the issue is not personal theology but accuracy in translation. Even non-Christian scholars of New Testament Greek would agree that the NWT is not accurate; after all, rules of languages, grammar, and translation are true regardless of personal theological belief.

20

What Are Some Examples of the *New World Translation* Mistranslation?

Watchtower literature offers strong warnings against those who would distort God's Word:

> Jehovah is against such clergy prophets whom he did not send forth from his intimate group and who "steal" words from his Bible in order to make a wrong application of them....he will rid himself of this "burden" by abandoning Christendom to calamity.... To such self-opinionated religionists, the Jeremiah class [Jehovah's Witnesses] say: "You have changed the words of the living God...."[220] God does not deal with persons who ignore his Word and go according to their own independent ideas.[221]

One wonders. If God would abandon "Christendom to calamity," for such alleged tampering with Scripture, what would He do with a group of religious leaders who actually committed such obstruction and then blamed the innocent? Who is it that really "steals" or "ignores" God's words in order to bolster their own independent ideas?

In the following section we have utilized the Watchtower Society's *New World Translation* (NWT) and their *Kingdom Interlinear Translation of the Greek Scriptures* (KIT). The latter gives the Greek text, a word-for-word English translation below the Greek text, and a column containing the NWT to the right. In the following examples we have provided the NWT and the New American Standard (NASB) translation so the reader may make a quick comparison prior to the discussion. A few of these discussions (John 1:1; Colossians 1:15-20) may be a bit technical. Some readers may wish to examine verses of particular interest and then move on.

Matthew 25:46. "Punishment," *kolasin,* is translated "cutting off" in order to escape the text's teaching of eternal punishment and to support their theology of annihilation of the wicked or conditional immortality.

> "And these will depart into everlasting CUTTING OFF but the righteous ones into everlasting life" (NWT).

> "And these will go away into eternal punishment, but the righteous into eternal life" (NASB).

How do standard Greek lexicons define *kolasin?* J. H. Moulton and G. Milligan in *The Vocabulary of the Greek New Testament* (Grand Rapids, MI: Eerdmans, 1980, p. 352) give an illustration of *kolasin* as "punishment and much torment." H.K. Moulton in *The Analytical Greek Lexicon Revised* (Grand Rapids, MI: Zondervan, 1978, p. 235) defines it as "chastisement, punishment." *New Thayer's Greek English Lexicon* (Wilmington, DE: Associated Publishers and Authors, 1974, 1977, p. 353) defines it as "correction, punishment, penalty." The *Arndt and Gingrich Greek-English Lexicon* (Chicago: University of Chicago, 1967, p. 441) states "1. punishment... 2. of divine retribution...go away into eternal punishment...." Gerhard Kittel (ed.), in the standard work *Theological Dictionary of New Testament* (Grand Rapids, MI: Eerdmans, 1978, Vol. 3, p. 816), defines it as "punishment."

Over hundreds of years, words may evolve in meaning; hence *kolasin* at one time could have been translated "cutting off," meaning the removal of that which is evil. It could also have the meaning of punishment for the purposes of correction.[222] But this was not its intended meaning in biblical times, as is evident from Greek scholars Mantey and Trench (Greek words are transliterated by the authors):

> In Jehovah's Witnesses' *New World Translation* and *Kingdom Interlinear Translation* (Matthew 25:46), the Greek word [*kolasin*], which is regularly defined as "punishment" in Greek lexicons, is translated "cutting-off," in spite of the fact that there isn't a

shred of lexical evidence anywhere for such a translation. We have found this word in first-century Greek writings in 107 different contexts and in every one of them, it has the meaning of "punishment," and never "cutting-off." But since their premise is that there can be no eternal punishment, they have translated the Scripture to make it somewhat compatible with their theology....*Kolasin* is also mistranslated "restraint" in 1 John 4:18.[223]

The [*kolasis aionios*] of Matthew xxv.46, as it is plain, is not merely corrective, and therefore temporary, discipline;...for in proof that [*kolasis*] with [*kolazesthai*] had acquired in Hellenistic Greek this severer sense, and was used simply as "punishment" or "torment," with no necessary underthought of the bettering through it of him who endured it, we have only to refer to such passages as the following: Josephus, Antt. xv. 2.2; Phil, De Agric. 9; Mart. Polycarp. 2; 2 Macc iv 38; Wisd. xix.4; and indeed the words of St. Peter himself (2 Peter ii.9).[224]

John 8:58. "I am" is translated "I have been" in order to circumvent Christ's deity.

"Jesus said to them: 'Most truly I say to you, before Abraham came into existence, I HAVE BEEN'" (NWT).

"Jesus said to them, 'Truly, truly, I say to you, before Abraham was born, I am'" (NASB).

The proper translation of the Greek *ego eimi* is "I am" not "I have been." This is a WS attempt to deny Christ's statement of deity (compare context) and to replace it with something compatible to the Witnesses' concept of Christ's limited preexistence. Dr. Mantey observes: "The translation of it as 'I have been' by Jehovah's Witnesses is wrong. The footnote stating that it is in 'the perfect indefinite tense' is also wrong. No Greek grammar, to my knowledge, has such a statement. In fact, there is no form *eimi* in the perfect tense in the Greek New Testament."[225]

It is also noteworthy that Michael Van Buskirk, author of *The Scholastic Dishonesty of the Watchtower,* has two official Watchtower Society letters showing that the Society has assumed four different grammatical positions in regard to *ego eimi:* a) "present indicative first person singular" (the correct designation); b) "a historical present"; c) the "perfect indefinite tense," but only "in a general sense"; and d) "perfect tense indicative."[226] But again, there is no "perfect indefinite tense" as they claim (see 1950, 1953 eds. of the NWT). Dr. Mantey also states that there is no "perfect indicative in this verse in Greek."[227] The correct answer is "present indicative, first person singular," which translates as "I am," not as "I have been." If the Watchtower Society had admitted (at least once) that the grammatical construction was a "present indicative, first person singular," why did they never translate it as such? In fact, one can look at their KIT (p. 467) and directly beneath the Greek *ego eimi* we find "I am"; but the translation column to the right reads "I have been."

Hebrews 9:27. This verse has the insertion of "for all time" to justify WS belief in conditional immortality.

> "And as it is reserved for men to die once FOR ALL TIME [eternally] but after this a judgment" (NWT).

> "And inasmuch as it is appointed for men to die once and after this comes judgment" (NASB).

Looking at the KIT (p. 988) we find the addition of the words "for all time" is without any justification. There is no Greek correspondence. Mantey states: "Hebrews 9:27, which without any grounds for it in the Greek, is mistranslated in the J. W. Translation....Note that the phrase 'for all time' was inserted in the former versions without any basis in the original for it. No honest scholar would attempt to so pervert the Word of God!"[228]

Luke 23:43. This verse inserts a comma after "today," to support their belief in soul sleep.

> "And he said to him: 'Truly I tell you today, You will [that is, later] be with me in Paradise'" (NWT).

> "And He said to him, 'Truly I say to you, today you shall be with Me in Paradise'" (NASB).

KIT (p. 408) admits that "in the original Greek no comma is found."

The noted commentator Lenski explains why the NWT is incorrect here:

> It should no longer be necessary to explain that "today" cannot be construed with "I say to thee." To be sure, Jesus is saying this today—when else would he be saying it? The adverb "today" is a necessary part of Jesus' promise to the malefactor. In fact, it has the emphasis. It would usually take three or four days until a man would die on the cross, so lingering was death by crucifixion. But Jesus assures this malefactor that his sufferings will cease "today." This is plain prophecy and at the same time blessed news to this sufferer. But Jesus says vastly more: "Today in company with me shalt thou be in Paradise!" This is an absolution. By this word Jesus acquits this criminal of sin and guilt.[229]

Matthew 27:50; Luke 23:46. The term "spirit" is translated as "breath" and/or "spirit" in order to support conditional immortality.

> "Again Jesus cried out with a loud voice, and yielded up (his) BREATH" (Matthew 27:50 NWT).

> "And Jesus cried out again with a loud voice, and yielded up His spirit" (Matthew 27:50 NASB).

> "And Jesus called with a loud voice and said 'Father into your hands I entrust my spirit.' When he had said

this he expired" (Luke 23:46 NWT). In this case "spirit" is translated correctly.

"And Jesus, crying out with a loud voice, said, 'Father, into Thy hands I commit My spirit.' And having said this, He breathed His last" (Luke 23:46 NASB).

In Matthew 27:50 *pneuma* (spirit) is mistranslated "breath" to support WS belief that no immortal spirit exists to be "yielded up." Yet Luke 23:46, the parallel account of this same event, which includes the actual cry of Jesus, shows that the translation "breath" is an impossible rendering, as it would have Jesus crying out, "Father, into Your hands I entrust my *breath*." The question is this: If in the NWT *pneuma* is translated "spirit" in Luke, why is it translated "breath" in the parallel passage in Matthew unless it is an obvious attempt to deny that Jesus' spirit continued after His physical death? Clearly, the Witnesses have distorted Matthew 27:50, although nothing could really be done by them with the passage in Luke.[230] KIT directly beneath the Greek translates "*pneuma*" as "spirit" in both places (pp. 168, 409). Why then not in both translations?

Acts 20:28. The phrase "with his own blood" is translated as "the blood of his own (Son)," to circumvent Christ's deity.

"Pay attention to yourselves and to all the flock, among which the holy spirit has appointed you overseers, to shepherd the congregation of God, which he purchased with THE BLOOD OF HIS OWN (SON)" (NWT).

"Be on guard for yourselves and for all the flock, among which the Holy Spirit has made you overseers, to shepherd the church of God which He purchased with His own blood" (NASB).

The KIT appendix justifying this translation (pp. 1160–61) refers to some manuscripts that use "Lord" (supposedly Jesus) instead of God and mentions "troublesome Greek words." It can offer this translation only by unnaturally translating the Greek, and it concludes, "The entire expression could therefore be translated 'with the blood of his own.'"[231]

Nigel Turner, an authority who wrote the volume on Greek syntax in Moulton's three-volume *Grammar of New Testament Greek*, explains why the Witnesses are wrong at this point:

> The dying proto-martyr, St. Stephen, addressed Jesus as if he were God. A pious Hellenistic Jew would not pray at one less than God. It may not be so generally appreciated that St. Paul slipped naturally and casually into the affirmation that he who shed his blood upon the cross was God. The reference is to Acts 20:28, where St. Paul at Miletus spoke to the Christian elders about "the church of God which he bought for himself by his own blood." The blood of God! Some aberrant manuscripts have the inoffensive reading, "the church of the Lord"—implying the Lord Jesus. But they must be rejected on the ground that the more startling or difficult reading is the one likely to be correct; scribes would not invent a conception of such unexpected originality as "the blood of God." We are left with the original and plain statement of St. Paul that Jesus is God, and it worries those scholars who think that it represents a Christology grammatical expedient whereby "his own" is understood as a noun ("his own One"), rather than a possessive adjective. In consequence, standing as it does in the genitive case, one may place before it the word "of": i.e., "of his Own." The expedient lowers the Christology drastically and reduces St. Paul's affirmation to something like this: "the church of God which he bought for himself by the blood of his Own"—as in the margin of the NEB. It is a theological expedient, foisting imaginary distinctions into a spontaneous affirmation, and is not the natural way to take the Greek. It is unlikely to have been the meaning envisaged either by St. Paul or the writer of the narrative.

The easy thing would be for them to add the word "Son," if that was intended.[232]

Even the KIT appendix admits,

> Grammatically, this passage could be translated, as in the King James Version and Douay Version, "with his own blood." In such case the verse would be saying that God purchased his congregation with his own blood. That has been a difficult thought with many...the ordinary translation would mean to say "God's blood."[233]

Nevertheless, the more accurate and natural translation is rejected since it cannot be true according to Watchtower theology, which denies the deity of Jesus Christ.

Hebrews 1:8. "Thy throne, O God" is translated "God is your throne" in order to circumvent Christ's deity.

> "But with the reference to the Son: 'GOD IS YOUR THRONE forever, and (the) scepter of your kingdom is the scepter of uprightness'" (NWT).

> "But of the Son He says, 'Thy throne, O God, is forever and ever, and the righteous scepter is the scepter of His kingdom'" (NASB).

Nigel Turner comments: "Happily in Hebrews 1:8 the NEB (New English Bible) no longer hesitates to accept in its text the statement that Jesus is God. 'Thy throne, O God, is for ever and ever.' It consigns to the margin the grotesque interpretation which obscures the godhead of Jesus ('God is thy throne for ever and ever')."[234]

Thomas Hewitt states,

> Some commentators have taken "O God" to be nominative, either subject or predicate. If subject, the translation would be "God is thy throne for ever and ever." If predicate "Thy throne is God," or "The foundation of thy throne is God." Such translations sound

very strange and have no parallel elsewhere. The AV, RV and RSV rightly support the vocative and translate "Thy throne, O God."...The Son, on the contrary, is addressed by the Father not as a messenger but as God, who occupies an eternal throne, and as Sovereign, who rules His Kingdom with righteousness.[235]

Former Rylands Professor of Biblical Criticism and Exegesis at the University of Manchester, F.F. Bruce, declares that here the "Messiah can be addressed not merely as God's Son (verse 5) but actually as God...."[236] As anyone can see, verse 10 corroborates that the intent of verse 8 is to declare Jesus as God (note the conjunction "and").

Colossians 1:15-20. These verses insert the word "other" in parenthesis in order to deny the eternal existence of Christ.

> "He is the image of the invisible God, the first-born of all creation; because by means of him all (OTHER) things were created in the heavens and upon the earth, the things visible and the things invisible, no matter whether they are thrones or lordships or governments or authorities. All (OTHER) things have been created through him and for him. Also, he is before all (OTHER) things and by means of him all (OTHER) things were made to exist, and he is the head of the body, the congregation. He is the beginning, the first-born from the dead, that he might become the one who is first in all things; because (God) saw good for all fullness to dwell in him, and through him to reconcile again to himself all (OTHER) things by making peace through the blood (he shed) on the torture stake, no matter whether they are the things upon the earth or the things in heaven" (NWT).

> "And He is the image of the invisible God, the first-born of all creation. For by Him all things were created, both in the heavens and on earth, visible and invisible,

whether thrones or dominions or rulers or authorities—all things have been created by Him and for
Him. And He is before all things, and in Him all
things hold together. He is also head of the body, the
church; and He is the beginning, the first-born from
the dead; so that He Himself might come to have first
place in everything. For it was the Father's good plea-
sure for all the fulness to dwell in Him, and through
Him to reconcile all things to Himself, having made
peace through the blood of His cross; through Him, I
say, whether things on earth or things in heaven"
(NASB).

In the NWT, the term "other" is inserted to imply that the
meaning of the passage is that Christ Himself is not *the* Creator.
We grant that a translator may insert a word in italics or brackets
if it is necessary to express the thought of the original accurately.
But even a cursory reading of the context here will show that
Christ *is* the Creator. KIT is again embarrassing itself (p. 896), for
it proves that the word "other" is not in the Greek. Yet this did not
prevent earlier editions of the NWT from using "other" *without*
brackets, implying that it was part of the Greek (see the 1950,
1953 eds.). Even the 1965 edition of *Make Sure of All things; Hold
Fast to That Which Is Fine* quotes Colossians 1:15-18 as if "other"
were part of the original Greek. No parenthetical brackets are present: "because by means of him all OTHER things were created....All OTHER things have been created through him and for
him."[237] In addition, modern versions of the NWT insert the word
"other" in Philippians 2:9, again changing the meaning ("the
name above every OTHER name"), and again without brackets or
italics, implying that it is in the original when in fact it is not, as
their own interlinear once again demonstrates.

Jehovah's Witnesses' objectivity cannot become more questionable than through examples of this type, where the Society
adds to the divine text what is simply not present in order to deny
what is clearly taught. Nevertheless, the Witnesses have somehow

overlooked John 1:3 (which the NWT translates correctly) that clearly declares the doctrine of Christ's deity, which they spuriously removed from Colossians: that if Christ is the Creator of *all* things, He Himself must be uncreated. The NWT translates John 1:3 as: "All things came into existence through him, and apart from him not even one thing came into existence."

While on the subject of Christ as Creator, Jehovah's Witnesses refer to the word *prototokos* ("first-born" in Colossians 1:15) as alleged evidence of Christ being "created." However, the word means priority and sovereignty over creation, as the context reveals. Bruce Metzger observes,

> Here he is spoken of as "the first begotten of all creation," which is something quite different from saying that he was made or created. If Paul had wished to express the latter idea, he had available a Greek word to do so, the word *protoktistos*, meaning "first created." Actually, however, Paul uses the *prototokes*, meaning "first begotten," which signifies something quite different, as the following explanation by a modern lay theologian makes clear:

> "One of the creeds says that Christ is the Son of God 'begotten, not created' and it adds 'begotten by his Father before all worlds.' Will you please get it quite clear that this has nothing to do with the fact that when Christ was born on earth as a man, that man was the son of a virgin? We are not now thinking about the Virgin Birth. We're thinking about something that happened before Nature was created at all, before time began. 'Before all worlds' Christ is begotten, not created. What does it mean?

> "We don't use the words *begetting* or *begotten* much in modern English, but everyone still knows what they mean. To beget is to become the father of: to create is to make. And the difference is just this. When you beget, you beget something of the same kind as

yourself. A man begets human babies, a beaver begets little beavers, and a bird begets eggs which turn into little birds. But when you make, you make something of a different kind from yourself. A bird makes a nest, a beaver builds a dam, a man makes a wireless set....Now that's the first thing to get clear.

"What God begets is God; just as what man begets is man. What God creates is not God; just as what man makes is not man."

To return now to Colossians 1:15 where Paul speaks of Christ as "the first begotten of all creation," it is important to observe that the adjective "first" refers both to rank as well as time. In other words, the Apostle alludes here not only to Christ's *priority* to all creation, but also to his *sovereignty* over all creation.[238]

One can mention other Scriptures. In Psalms 89:27, "first-born" clearly means preeminence. In Jeremiah 31:9, Ephraim is the "first-born" although Manasseh was literally born first; hence "first-born" must refer to rank or preeminence.

Colossians 2:9. In this verse "deity" is translated as "divine quality" in order to circumvent Christ's deity.

"...because it is in him that all the fullness of the DIVINE QUALITY dwells bodily" (NWT).

"For in Him all the fulness of Deity dwells in bodily form" (NASB).

The great grammarian, A.T. Robertson, author of *A Grammar of the Greek New Testament,* declares,

In this sentence...Paul states the heart of his message about the Person of Christ. There dwells (at home) in Christ not one or more aspects of the Godhead (the very essence of God, from *theos, deitas*) and not to be confused with *theiotes* in Romans 1:20 (from *theios,* the quality of God, *divinitas*), here only in N. T. as *theiotes* only in Romans 1:20. The distinction is observed in Lucian and Plutarch. *Theiotes* occurs in the papyri and inscriptions. Paul here asserts that "all the pleroma (fullness) of the Godhead," not just certain aspects, dwells in Christ and in bodily form...dwells now in Christ in his glorified humanity....He asserts plainly the deity and the humanity of Jesus Christ in corporeal form.[239]

Metzger asserts:

Nothing could be clearer or more emphatic than this declaration. It means that everything without exception which goes to make the godhead, or divine quality, dwells or resides in Jesus Christ bodily, that is, is invested with a body in Jesus Christ. It is to be noticed also that Paul uses the present tense of the verb, "dwells." He does not say that the fullness of the divine quality "has dwelt" in Jesus Christ, but that it "dwells" there.[240]

Gruss concurs:

The word *theotes* is here translated "divine quality" which is not a literal or correct rendering. Grimm-Thayer gave as the meaning of this word, "*deity* i.e., the state of being God, Godhead: Colossians ii. 9." The word for "divinity" or "divine character" is found in Romans 1:20 and is *theiotes* which is rendered by Grimm-Thayer as "divinity, divine nature." Cremer gives "the Godhead" as the meaning of *theotes* and then says that the two words are to be distinguished: "*theotes*—that which God is, *theiotes*—that which is of God." In the discussion of these two words Trench writes concerning Colossians 2:9:

"...St. Paul is declaring that in the Son there dwells all the fullness of absolute Godhead: they were no mere rays of divine glory which gilded Him lighting up his

person for a season and with a splendour not his own;
but He was, and is, absolute and perfect God...."[241]

Titus 2:13; 2 Peter 1:1. (Compare Ephesians 5:5; 2 Thessalonians 1:12.) In these verses "our great God and Savior" is translated as "the great God and the Savior" in order to deny Christ's deity.

> "...while we wait for the happy hope and glorious manifestation of the great God AND OF (THE) Savior of us, Christ Jesus" (Titus 2:13 NWT).

> "...looking for the blessed hope and the appearing of the glory of our great God and Savior, Christ Jesus" (Titus 2:13 NASB).

The Greek of Titus 2:13 and 2 Peter 1:1 is very similar, with *megalou,* "great," being absent in 2 Peter.

The NWT changes the proper translation to separate Jesus Christ from the term God, thereby denying His deity. In the NWT, the verse is translated as if two persons are being spoken of, God and Jesus, rather than one person only, Jesus Christ. This violates a rule of Greek grammar called the Granville Sharp rule. In simplified form it states that when two singular personal nouns (a personal noun is distinguished from a proper noun in this rule) of the same case ending (God and Savior, genitive case) are connected by "and" (*kai*) and only the first noun has the modifying article "the" (*tou*) (the second noun does not), it always means that both nouns uniformly refer to the same person. When defined properly, the rule has no exceptions in the New Testament.[242] John Weldon remembers being challenged publicly, at this point, by a Greek expert concerning his "error" regarding the universality of Granville Sharp, which illustrates that even otherwise well-informed people can be in error concerning this rule.

Thus "God" and "Savior" must both refer to one person, to Jesus, in Titus 2:13 and 2 Peter 1:1. In fact, in ancient times the same phraseology ("god and savior") was used of a ruling king.

These two verses, then, must be translated as "our great God and Savior Jesus Christ."[243]

The KIT explanation for the WS translation (p. 1163) is typically biased, sounding scholarly but misquoting Moulton's *Grammar,* as we will later document. In *A Manual Grammar of the Greek New Testament,* Dana and Mantey state: "The following rule by Granville Sharp of a century back still proves to be true:... 2 Peter 1:1...means that Jesus is our God and Savior. After the same manner Titus 2:13...asserts that Jesus is the great God and Savior."[244] (The reason why the King James Version, the American Standard Version, and a few additional earlier versions incorrectly translate such passages is, in part, according to Robertson, due to the influence of the grammatical work of George B. Winer.)[245]

John 1:1. "God" is translated as "a god" in order to deny Christ's deity.

> "In (the) beginning the Word was, and the Word was with God, and the Word was a god" (NWT).

> "In the beginning was the Word, and the Word was with God, and the Word was God" (NASB).

The transliterated Greek of this verse looks like this:

> *En arche en ho logos kai ho logos*
> In beginning was the Word and the Word

> *en pros ton theon kai theos en ho logos*
> was toward the God and God was the Word

In essence, the Watchtower Society, violating another rule of Greek grammar, Colwell's Rule, claims that it can translate *theos* as "a god" because there is no definite article before this usage of *theos* (God) in the last clause of John 1:1. Note that the first use (*pros ton theon*) has the article (*ton,* "the"). The second use simply states *kai theos,* "and God," (not "and the God"). Because it does not say "and *the* God," Jehovah's Witnesses argue that they are free to interpret this second usage of "God" as, figuratively, meaning a lesser deity, "a god," a designation signifying Christ's exalted status, even though He is still only a creature.

The WS concern here is to escape the clear and forceful meaning of this passage, in which Christ is called *theos,* God. But had the apostle John used the article, he would have declared "*the* God was the Word." Had he done so, he would have confused the persons of the Trinity and supported modalism (in the early church this was known as the heresy of Sabellianism). In other words, to say that "*the* God was the Word (Jesus)" would have declared that all of God, the whole trinity, was Jesus. This would have supported modern modalistic belief as well that there is only one Person in the Godhead (Jesus, that is, "Jesus only") and that the terms Father, Son, and Spirit in Scripture only refer to modes or offices of the God who exists as one person.

The apostle John had to make a finer distinction and, on the one hand, clearly declare that the person of Jesus was deity but, on the other hand, not make it seem as if all three persons in the Godhead were to be considered the same as the person of Jesus. To make this fine distinction he had to use the exact wording he used.

We should note that KIT (pp. 1158–59) utilizes both Mantey's and Robertson's *Grammar* in defense of their John 1:1 translation. However, Dr. Mantey publicly rebuked them:

> Since my name is used and our [Dana & Mantey] *Manual Grammar of the Greek New Testament* is quoted on page 744 to seek to justify their translation, I am making this statement...of all the scholars in the world, as far as we know none have translated this verse as Jehovah's Witnesses have done. If the Greek article occurred with both Word and God in John 1:1, the implication would be that they are one and the same person, absolutely identical. But John affirmed that "the Word was with (the) God" (the definite article preceding each noun), and in so writing, he indicated his belief that they are distinct and separate

> personalities. Then John next stated that the Word
> was God, i.e., of the same family or essence that char-
> acterizes the Creator. Or, in other words, that both are
> of the same nature, and that nature is the highest in
> existence, namely divine....The apostle John, in the
> context of the introduction to his Gospel, is pulling
> all the stops out of language to portray not only the
> deity of Christ, but also his equality with the Father.
> He states that the Word was in the beginning, that He
> was with God, that He was God and that all creation
> came into existence through him and that not even
> one thing exists that was not created by Christ. What
> else could be said that John did not say?[246]

As for Dr. Robertson, the WS misstates his position by selectively quoting him. As they observe, Robertson does say that "the
absence of the article here is on purpose." But Jehovah's Witnesses
do not explain *why* Robertson says this. He does so to indicate
that to include the article "would have been Sabellianism."[247] In his
Word Pictures, Robertson provides a succinct analysis:

> By exact and careful language John denied Sabel-
> lianism by not saying *ho theos enho logos* (the God
> was the Word). That would mean that all of God was
> expressed in *ho logos* (the Word) and the terms would
> be interchangeable, each having the article. The sub-
> ject is made plain by the article (*ho logos*) and the
> predicate without it (*theos*) just as in John 4:24
> *pneuma ho theos* can only mean "God is spirit," not
> "spirit is God." So in I John 4:16 *ho theos agape estin*
> can only mean "God is love," not "love is God" as a so-
> called Christian scientist would confusedly say. For
> the article with the predicate see Robertson,
> *Grammar,* pp. 767f. So in John 1:14 *ho Logos sarx
> egeneto,* "the Word became flesh," not "the flesh
> became Word."[248]

The Watchtower Society appendix defending their rendering "a
god" (KIT, pp. 1158–60) appears scholarly but is not. For example,

they misquote Dana and Mantey's *Grammar*. In a letter dated July 11, 1974, to the WS, Mantey demanded a public apology for their repeated misquotings (in millions of printings), and he requested their discontinuance of the use of his grammar. (See the Appendix.)

A related argument the WS uses here is given as follows: "At Acts 28:6 we have a case paralleling that of John 1:1 with exactly the same predicate construction, namely, with an anarthrous [no definite article] ΘΕΟΣ [*theos*]" (KIT, p. 1160). This at first seems to be true, for there is no definite article in Acts 28:6. What the Witnesses fail to mention is that in John 1:1 the predicate nominative (*theos*) precedes the verb, but in Acts it follows the verb and thus is not applicable. Colwell's rule, which is at issue here, states that a definite predicate nominative has the article when it follows the verb and lacks the article when it precedes it:

> Such a rendering is a frightful mistranslation. It overlooks entirely an established rule of Greek grammar which necessitates the rendering, "...and the Word was God." Some years ago Dr. Ernest Cadman Colwell of the University of Chicago pointed out in a study of the Greek definite article that, "A definite predicate nominative has the article when it follows the verb; it does not have the article when it precedes the verb.... In a lengthy Appendix in the Jehovah's Witnesses' translation, which was added to support the mistranslation of John 1:1, there are quoted thirty-five other passages in John where the predicate noun has the definite article in Greek. These are intended to prove that the absence of the article in John 1:1 requires that ΘΕΟΣ must be translated "a god." None of the thirty-five instances is parallel, however, for in every case the predicate noun stands after the verb, and so, according to Colwell's rule, properly has the article. So far, therefore, from being evidence against the usual translation of John 1:1, these instances add confirmation to the full enunciation of the rule of the

Greek definite article. Furthermore, the additional references quoted in the New World Translation from the Greek of the Septuagint translation of the Old Testament, in order to give further support to the erroneous rendering in the opening verse of John, are exactly in conformity with Colwell's rule, and therefore are added proof of the accuracy of the rule. The other passages adduced in the Appendix are, for one reason or another, not applicable to the question at issue. (Particularly inappropriate is the reference to Acts 28:6, for no one has ever maintained that the pagan natives of Malta regarded Paul as anything other than "a god.")[249]

Van Buskirk points out that the Witnesses have attempted to deny Colwell's Rule by misquoting Phillip B. Harner's article in *Journal of Biblical Literature*, "Qualitative Anarthrous Predicate Nouns: Mark 15:39 and John 1:1" (Vol. 92, 1973, p. 87). However, a full *year* earlier Dr. Mantey sent a letter to the Watchtower Society demanding they stop misquoting him. He pointed out that not only had they misquoted Colwell's Rule but also that it is impossible to quote Harner in denial of Colwell since Harner himself supports the rule and denies the possibility of an "a god" translation. Van Buskirk observes: "One's mind staggers at the depths to which someone will sink to prove his point. In the Watchtower's case both Colwell and Harner show that in John 1:1 'a god' is not a permissible translation. Yet without blinking an eye they will quote, out of context, the man who refutes them. Harner's article in no way concludes what the Watchtower makes it conclude in their letter."[250] (Van Buskirk goes on to discuss exactly what Harner concluded and how his research is complementary to Colwell's; it simply brings out new information.)

Nevertheless, even if we were to assume the truth of what the Watchtower Society claims in their KIT appendix, they have violated their own John 1:1 "rule" 94 percent of the time. Robert H. Countess, writing in *The Jehovah's Witnesses' New Testament*, documents this in detail.[251] In John 1 alone they violate their principle at least five times. Checking their interlinear (pp. 417–19), we see the following: John 1:6 *para theou*—no definite article; John 1:12 *tekna theou*—no definite article; John 1:13 *ek theou*—no definite article; John 1:18 *Theon*—no definite article; John 1:23 *odon Kuriou*—no definite article.

If, according to WS standards, the absence of the article demands the rendering "a god," why do they not so render it here? In fact, where is it in 94 percent of the instances of such construction in the NWT? Clearly, translating John 1:1 as saying "a god" is not only a violation of Greek grammar but also unjustified even in light of the vast majority of their own translation. Obviously, then, in the preceding passages and in John 1:1, the translation should be "God," not "a god." (As an aside, the NWT at John 1:23 translates the Greek *kurios* [Lord] as "Jehovah," because it is a clear reference to Jehovah God from Isaiah. Yet, according to their John 1:1 rendering, with no definite article, it should be "a Jehovah." If "a god" must be different from God, "a Jehovah" must then be different from Jehovah. At this point we would have three "Gods": "Jehovah," "a god," and "a Jehovah.")

Philippians 1:23. The word "depart" is translated as "releasing" to support a belief in soul sleep.

> "I am under pressure from these two things; but what I do desire is the RELEASING and the being with Christ" (NWT).

> "But I am hard-pressed from both directions, having the desire to depart and be with Christ, for that is very much better" (NASB).

Dr. Walter Martin commented, "The rendering, 'but what I do desire is the releasing,' particularly the last word, is a gross imposition upon the principles of Greek exegesis because the untutored Russellites have rendered the first aorist active infinitive of the verb *analuoo* (*analusai*) as a substantive (the releasing), which in this context is unscholarly and atrocious Greek. In order to translate it 'the releasing' the form would have to be the participle construction (*analusas*)."[252] (Martin also shows that in 2 Timothy 4:6 the Witnesses accept the similar form of the same word as meaning "death," but they cannot do so in Philippians 1:23 for reasons of theological bias.)

Matthew 24:3. The word "coming" is translated as "presence" to justify the "invisible presence" of Jesus since 1914.

> "Tell us, when will these things be, and what will be the sign of your PRESENCE and of the conclusion of the system of these things?" (NWT).

> "Tell us, when will these things be, and what will be the sign of Your coming, and of the end of the age?" (NASB).

The Greek word *parousia*, according to its context, should be translated "coming." (It can be translated "presence," but context must determine which is correct.) As Martin pointed out,

> Jehovah's Witnesses claim scholarship for this blanket translation of *parousia*, yet not one great scholar in the history of Greek exegesis and translation has ever held this view. Since 1871, when Pastor Russell produced this concept, upon examination, it has been denounced by every competent scholar. The reason this Russellite rendering is so dangerous is that it attempts to prove that *parousia*, in regard to Christ's second advent, really means that His return or "presence" was to be invisible and unknown to all but "the faithful" (Russellites, of course)....To conclude that presence necessarily implies invisibility is also another flaw in the Watchtower's argument, for in numerous places where they render parousia "presence," the persons spoken of were hardly invisible. (See 1 Corinthians 16:17; 2 Corinthians 7:6; and 10:10.)[253]

In the *New Thayer's Greek-English Lexicon* we find these comments under the word *parousia*: "In the N.T., esp. of the advent, i.e., the future, visible, return from heaven of Jesus, the Messiah, to raise the dead, hold the last judgment, and set up formally and gloriously the kingdom of God: Matthew 24:3."[254]

Over 200 verses: the translation of YHWH as "Jehovah." We can see biased translations even in the Witnesses' own term "Jehovah," which is so important to them as allegedly signifying the "true" name of God. The NWT adds "Jehovah" to the New Testament text over 200 times, in spite of the fact that "Jehovah" is not found anywhere in the Bible, New or Old Testament. WS claims that the New Testament originals were "tampered with," and that the tetragrammaton (YHWH) was surreptitiously removed, substituting *kurios* (Lord) and *theos* (God).

The truth is that YHWH never occurs in any New Testament Greek manuscript, and it occurs in only one Septuagint copy.[255] There is simply no evidence of tampering.[256] The Old Testament YHWH itself can be translated different ways, since the insertion of vowels is arbitrary. YHWH could have been Jehovah, or JiHiViH or JaHiVeH and so on. In other words, the translation of the Greek words *kurios* (God) and (Lord) *theos* as JEHOVAH in the NWT (some 237 times) is a completely unjustified translation. We simply do not know the "true" name of God. Metzger observes: "The introduction of the word 'Jehovah' into the New Testament text, in spite of much ingenuity in an argument filled with a considerable amount of irrelevant material (pp. 10–25), is a plain piece of special pleading."[257]

There is another reason for the WS use of "Jehovah" in place of "Lord"; it thereby denies the deity of Christ where the term "Lord" (applied to Jesus) connotes the meaning of Jehovah in the Old Testament. Often, when the New Testament refers to Christ as "Lord," it is associating Him with Jehovah in the Old Testament. The Watchtower Society has had to be inconsistent in its translation, translating *kurios* variously as "Jehovah" or "Lord" to suit their own theology. For example, if we look at KIT (p. 723) for

Romans 10:11, *kurios* is translated "Lord," but in verse 13 the same word, which here clearly refers to Jesus, is now translated "Jehovah" rather than "Lord" or "Jesus." In both places the term "Lord" refers to Jesus and connotes His deity, but the NWT hides this by the translation of "Lord" in verse 11 and "Jehovah" in verse 13, implying that the entire section refers to Jehovah, but not to Jesus. Likewise, Philippians 2:10-11 clearly refers to Jesus and is based on Isaiah 45:22-25, referring to Jehovah (see Romans 14:9-11). If *kurios* were translated "Jehovah" in Philippians 2, it would mean that Jesus is identified with Jehovah, and the Watchtower Society could not permit such a translation. Hence, *kurios* is here translated "Lord," not Jehovah. Thus, it is only where *kurios* can be translated Jesus and simultaneously *not* imply His deity, that it is so translated.

Additional examples. Professor Gruss observes a number of other errors in WS translation.[258] In Matthew 24:6,14; 1 Peter 4:7; 2 Corinthians 11:15; Revelation 19:20, and elsewhere words are added that are not in the Greek. And despite the WS claim not to engage in paraphrasing, the NWT repeatedly paraphrases when Scripture refers to believers being "in Christ." *All* believers everywhere can be in Christ only if Jesus is God. But in the NWT, the term "in" (Greek *en*), "in Christ," is often mistranslated, such as "in union with" (Christ) or something similar. The Witnesses then interpret this to mean a union of purpose rather than a spiritual union. Gruss comments: "With the same Greek word being translated properly in every case except when it refers to the believer's personal relationship with Christ, it must be concluded that the translator's paraphrasing is nothing less than interpretation. One loses confidence in a translation which professes to be literal when it is replete with biased paraphrases."[259]

In Philippians 3:11 the Greek *exanastasis* (resurrection) is erroneously translated "earlier resurrection." And in John 13:18; 17:12; 19:24,36, the exact same Greek words are translated four different ways. Robert H. Countess refers to additional mistranslations.[260]

In light of such examples, our only conclusion is that the Watchtower Bible and Tract Society (WBTS) can hardly be concerned with accurately translating the New Testament.

So far we have referred to the New Testament portion of the *New World Translation*. What of the Old Testament? Although space does not permit illustrations, according to reviewers it is not much improved. British scholar H.H. Rowley asserts, "From beginning to end this volume is a shining example of how the Bible should not be translated…" and he calls it "an insult to the Word of God."[261] Gruss points out that the WS translation of the Old Testament has the same basic purpose as that of the New, to justify preconceived Watchtower theology.[262]

We should emphasize again that our analysis of the *New World Translation* here is not a result of "biased trinitarian theology," as Witnesses are fond of claiming. If the scholars quoted above are biased, it is toward a respect for rules of grammar and divine revelation. A Christian should feel free to challenge a Witness by appealing to non-Christian authorities at this point. Any university Greek professor could be consulted for his view of the *New World Translation* at John 1:1, Matthew 25:46, and so on.

Since the Watchtower Society has failed the test of accurately translating the Bible, it cannot claim adherence to or a respect for divine revelation. Can it then be considered the only channel through which God has chosen to operate on earth?

21

What Does the Watchtower Society Teach Concerning the Definition and Interpretation of Biblical Prophecy?

By establishing the Watchtower Society's definition and view of prophecy, we will be able to establish whether the WS meets its own standards for prophetic fulfillment. The *Watchtower* of March 1, 1975, declares, "The Bible itself establishes the rules for testing a prophecy at Deuteronomy 18:20-22 and 13:1-8."[263] In Deuteronomy 18, the Bible states that prophets who presume, falsely, to speak in God's name that which He never commanded them to speak shall be put to death (18:20), and also that: "If what a prophet proclaims in the name of the LORD does not take place or come true, that is a message the LORD has not spoken. That prophet has spoken presumptuously. Do not be afraid of him" (18:22). In Deuteronomy 13 we are warned that if a prophet does a miracle but tells people to follow false gods, he must be put to death, because he is a false prophet in spite of displaying a miracle. Although the historical contexts differ in the following verses, the principle remains. God Himself declares the prophet is "recognized as one truly sent by the LORD *only* if his prediction comes true" (Jeremiah 28:9, emphasis added), because "whatever I say will be fulfilled, declares the Sovereign LORD" (Ezekiel 12:28). The biblical standard is clear.

Note further that the Watchtower Society's *Aid to Bible Understanding* states that prophecy includes "a declaration of something to come," that "the source of all true prophecy is Jehovah God," and that "correct understanding of prophecy would still be made available by God...particularly in the foretold 'time of the end'"[264] (a reference to the alleged relevance of the Watchtower Society). A "prophet" is defined as "one through whom the divine will and purpose are made known," which reflects the claims of the Watchtower Society for itself.[265] Also, we are told that "the three essentials for establishing the credentials of the true prophet" are 1) speaking in Jehovah's name, 2) that "the things foretold would come to pass," and 3) promoting true worship by being in harmony with God's already revealed word.[266] The true prophet "expressed God's mind on matters....Every prediction related to God's will, purpose, standards or judgment."[267]

In light of these claims, the WS has little room in which to wiggle, for it claims to speak in the name of Jehovah, to be His prophet predicting future events, to predict those events accurately, and to be in harmony with His Word. In the September 1,

1979, *Watchtower,* the Society declares that "for nearly 60 years now [since Rutherford's post-1918 era] the Jeremiah class have faithfully spoken forth Jehovah's Word."[268] Clearly, then, "the things foretold (would) come to pass." But have they? No, they have not—not even once!

The Jehovah's Witnesses are thus confronted with an insurmountable predicament. Yet many fail to recognize the depth of the quandary. John Weldon remembers a three-hour discussion he and a friend had with two Jehovah's Witnesses, one of whom had the reputation of being one of their best apologists. The apologist was shown numerous false prophecies in the *Watchtower* magazine. It hardly seemed to bother him. He admitted, "There have been some errors in prophetic interpretation." While he was willing to accept "a few" genuine errors, he entirely ignored the implications. We have two points in response.

First, divine guidance is divine guidance. The Watchtower Society claims to be God's prophet and His *only* channel on earth for disseminating divine truth. This includes the "true interpretation" of the Bible and disclosing true and relevant prophetic information on a regular basis. Based on the Society's acceptance of biblical standards and its own claims for accuracy, one should expect an inerrant record. If the Watchtower is divinely guided in the manner it claims to be, inerrancy is the proof of their claims. Even "a few errors" nullify WS claims to genuine divine guidance. And if the Society's leadership admits that it is incapable of accurately receiving or interpreting such guidance, this in effect nullifies the very claim, for guidance must be accurate if it is to have any value. Imagine the Pentagon informing Congress that a 100-billion-dollar missile tracking system is 100 percent accurate, but then informing Congress that they can give no assurance that military officers will be able to interpret the tracking accurately.

Second, we are not dealing here with "a few" or "some" errors of biblical prophecy. We are dealing with *hundreds* of prophetic errors. These have proliferated from the start of the WS, and they continue to this day. This is why the issue of false prophecy ought to be so relevant to the average Witness—because it represents a *continual pervasive pattern* in Watchtower history, not just an exception "here and there" which blemishes an otherwise perfect record. In other words, as with the biases of their Bible translation, the Watchtower prophetic record is one of repeated failure without even marginal success. It is this fact that the average Witness must come to grips with.

Further, WS leadership *knows* the dismal record of failure—how could they not? Former leader Raymond Franz wrote in *Crisis of Conscience:*

> During the first twenty years or so of my active association with Jehovah's Witnesses, I had at most a hazy idea about any failures in past predictions and simply did not attach any great importance to them....It was not until the late 1970s that I learned just how far the matter went. I learned it then, not from so-called "opposition literature," but from Watchtower publications themselves and from active and respected Witnesses, including members of the Governing Body of Jehovah's Witnesses.[269]

How can such a fact possibly be reconciled with *any* claim to divine guidance? Further, if God had been guiding the Watchtower Society, and if they had been receiving this guidance accurately, then they have a much more serious problem than if they claimed no guidance, for God would, obviously, be neither omnipotent nor omniscient.

If the Watchtower cannot be trusted in prophecy, if they have misperceived the "holy spirit's" guidance here, how can anyone be assured they have not misperceived "its" guidance elsewhere, as in critical doctrinal teachings? If they are fallible at one point, they are potentially fallible at any point. Given their penchant for biased translation and exegesis, deliberate cover-up of earlier errors, and other dubious matters, one can argue that the WS should not be trusted in any area.

22
_____

DOES THE WATCHTOWER SOCIETY CLEARLY CLAIM DIVINE GUIDANCE IN ITS PROPHETIC MINISTRY?

If we thoroughly document the pervasive nature of WS claims to divine guidance, the extent of prophetic failure will be underscored beyond doubt. These claims are established by: 1) claims to prophethood, 2) claims to guidance from "holy spirit" or angels, and 3) other direct claims to divine guidance.

Claims to prophethood

The Jehovah's Witnesses are collectively held to be a "prophet" of God and to receive divine guidance from Jehovah through the Watchtower Society and its publications. The WS, then, is the true prophet who distributes Jehovah's prophecies to the faithful for dissemination to others. Here are some examples from WS literature:

> *The Nations Shall Know that I Am Jehovah—How?* (1971): [Jehovah's Witnesses] serve as the mouthpiece...of Jehovah [and] speak as a prophet in the name of Jehovah....(pp. 58–59).

> The *Watchtower*, November 1, 1956: Who controls the organization, who directs it?...the living God Jehovah (p. 666).

> The *Watchtower*, April 1, 1972: These questions can be answered in the affirmative. Who is this prophet?... This "prophet" was not one man, but was a body of men and women. It was the small group of footstep followers of Jesus Christ, known at that time as International Bible Students. Today they are known as Jehovah's Christian witnesses....Of course, it is easy to say that this group acts as a "prophet" of God. It is another thing to prove it. The only way that this can be done is to review the record. What does it show? (p. 197).

Jehovah is interested not only in the vindication of his own name but also in vindicating his "prophet" (p. 200).

The book *Holy Spirit* declares that the Witnesses have been "prophesying from house to house" and "prophesying to all the nations."[270]

Claims to guidance from "holy spirit" or angels

This was established earlier. The WS receives guidance from Jehovah and Jesus through "angels." In the *Watchtower* April 1, 1972, we read: "This would indicate that Jehovah's witnesses today make their declaration of the good news of the Kingdom under angelic direction and support (Revelation 14:6-7; Matthew 25:31-32)." "And since no word or work of Jehovah can fail, for he is God Almighty, the nations will see the fulfillment of what these witnesses say as directed from heaven" (p. 200). The *Watchtower* of July 1, 1973, states: "Jehovah's organization alone, in all the earth, is directed by God's holy spirit or active force....To it alone God's Sacred Word, the Bible, is not a sealed book" (p. 402).

Other direct claims to divine guidance

Judge Rutherford implied that his books and the Watchtower publications were "the word of God" (the *Watchtower,* April 1, 1932). Other WS publications from that era state:

> The *Watchtower,* December 1, 1933: "No man is given credit for the wonderful truths which the Lord has revealed to his people through the Watch Tower publications" (p. 263).

> The 1934, 1935, and 1936 *Yearbooks,* respectively: "All credit and honor are due to the Lord for what appears in the Watchtower" (p. 69).

> "It is the privilege of the Watchtower to publish explanation of the prophecies....There is no attempt on the part of the Watchtower to interpret prophecy, for the reason that no human creature can interpret prophecy" (p. 52).

"No human creature is entitled to any credit for what appears in the Watchtower" (p. 63).

The *Watchtower,* February 1, 1938, Vol. LIX, No. 3: "All this information came not from or by man, but by the Lord God" (p. 35).

The *Watchtower,* January 1, 1942: "Those who are convinced that the Watchtower is publishing the opinion or expression of a man should not waste time looking at it at all" (p. 5).

The *Watchtower,* April 15, 1943: "*The Watchtower* is a magazine without equal in the earth....The getting of correct information and instruction, just such as is required for the times...was never more vital than now....This is not giving any credit to the magazine's publishers, but is due to the great Author of the Bible with its truths and prophecies, and who now interprets its prophecies" (p. 129).

Judge Rutherford authored every Jehovah's Witness book from 1926 to 1942 and supervised virtually everything that went into the *Watchtower* magazine. The claims here are clear: Rutherford received divine inspiration/revelation, and it was impossible to understand any biblical passage unless one was reading one of Rutherford's books that explained it, which is precisely the claim of the Watchtower Society today with its own literature.

The 1950 edition of the *New World Translation of the Christian Greek Scriptures* carried an advertisement on page 793 for the *Watchtower* magazine where it was declared to be "a dependable Bible study aid," and that "since 1879...the Watchtower has consistently proved itself dependable." With all these claims, and many more, can anyone logically doubt that if they are true, then the WS must have a virtually perfect prophetic record?*

---

* When Russell or Rutherford expressed such sentiments as "we have never claimed inspiration or prophetic vision,"[271] they were self-deceived, engaging in rationalization or lying, because as we just saw, this is exactly what they expressed in different terminology.

The following cases represent only a sampling; the actual number of false prophecies is far greater. Unless otherwise noted, all statements are taken from the *Watchtower*. We should remember that the average Jehovah's Witness does not look forward to the Second Coming of Christ, because according to the WS this has already occurred; rather, they look forward to the Battle of Armageddon, which will end with the ushering in of the new millennium and a paradise on earth. Hence, most prophecies deal with the coming battle of Armageddon.

23

WHAT ARE SOME OF THE FALSE PROPHECIES DECLARED BY THE WATCHTOWER SOCIETY?

Will you speak what is unjust for God, and speak what is deceitful for Him? (Job 13:7 NASB).

The Failure of the 1914 prediction

Jehovah's Witnesses repeatedly prophesied 1914 as the year to mark the end of the battle of Armageddon and the beginning of the millennial reign. As early as 1877, warnings were being given of the imminent end of the world:

> 1877—THE END OF THIS WORLD… is nearer than most men suppose.[272]

> 1889—In subsequent chapters we present proofs that the setting up of the Kingdom of God is already begun….And that the "battle of the great day of God Almighty" (Revelation 16:14), which will end in A.D. 1914 with the complete overthrow of earth's present rulership, is already commenced.[273] [The 1915 edition of this book changed "A.D. 1914" to "A.D. 1915."]

> July 15, 1894—We see no reason for changing the futures—nor could we change them if we would.

They are, we believe, God's dates, not ours. But bear in mind that the end of 1914 is not the date for the *beginning,* but for the *end* of the time of trouble. We see no reason for changing from our opinion expressed in the view presented in the WATCH TOWER of January 15, '92. We advise that it be read again. [First emphasis added.][274]

1904—The stress of the great time of trouble will be on us soon, somewhere between 1910 and 1912—culminating with the end of the "Times of the Gentiles," October, 1914.[275]

May 1, 1914—There is absolutely no ground for Bible students to question that the consummation of this Gospel age is now even at the door....The great crisis...that will consume the ecclesiastical heavens and the social earth, is very near.[276]

The year 1914 ended without a single prediction of Russell's coming true.[277] Before we comment further, let us also note that Russell did not predict a *spiritual* fulfillment in 1914, as modern Jehovah's Witnesses claim; that is, he did not predict that Jesus would set up His kingdom in *heaven.* Russell predicted a physical kingdom on earth. But modern Jehovah's Witnesses have denied that the original prediction was earthly. Referring to Jehovah's Witnesses in 1880, modern Witnesses claim that the earlier Witnesses predicted a *heavenly* kingdom: "In the 'Watchtower' magazine of March, 1880, they said: 'The Times of the Gentiles extend to 1914, and the heavenly kingdom will not have full sway till then.' Of all people, only the witnesses pointed to 1914 as the year for God's kingdom to be fully set up in heaven."[278] But let us go back to the March, 1880, *Zion's Watch Tower* (the original name of the *Watchtower* magazine), where we find the original prophecy, which is only quoted in part above. *Zion's Watch Tower* for March 1880 carries the full quote. In the Reprint Index, this very article is included under the title "*earthly* kingdom" (p. 6569). The original material clearly referred to an earthly, not a heavenly, rule:

> The "Times of the Gentiles" extend to 1914, and the
> heavenly kingdom will not have full sway till then, but
> as a "Stone" the kingdom of God is set up "*in the days*
> of these (ten gentile) kings," and by consumating [sic]
> them it becomes a universal kingdom—a "great
> mountain and fills the whole Earth."[279]

For Russell, "the heavenly kingdom" "fills the whole *Earth.*"
Further, Russell's third volume of *Studies in the Scriptures* (1891)
declared that there would exist "the full establishment of the
Kingdom of God *in the earth* at A.D. 1914."[280] In another book
published in 1899, he stated that he would "prove that *before that
date* [1914; emphasis his] God's Kingdom, organized in power,
will be *in the earth,*" and that before the end of 1914: a) the last
member of the church of Christ would be glorified, b) Jerusalem
and Israel would be restored to divine favor, c) there would be "a
worldwide reign of anarchy," and d) the Kingdom of the world
would be destroyed.[281] By the end of 1914, none of these predictions came true.

Like false prophets generally, Russell was undaunted by his
failure and continued to supply additional false prophecies. The
April 1, 1915, issue of *Zion's Watch Tower*[282] referred to the faithful
taking "the Bible view of the Great Armageddon, of which we are
now having the prelude," and "the battle of Armageddon to which
this war [World War I] is leading." In the September 1, 1916, issue
he continued to hope: "We see no reason for doubting, therefore,
that the Times of the Gentiles ended in October, 1914; and that a
few more years will witness their utter collapse and the full establishment of God's kingdom in the hands of Messiah."[283] This
prophecy (the "few more years") also failed. Gruss further points
out that the WS is incorrect in claiming that Russell at least predicted World War I.[284] To the contrary, Russell only confirmed his
own status as a false prophet. Listen to Russell's own words eight
years prior in the *Watchtower* of October 1, 1907:[285]

> But let us suppose a case far from our expectations.…
> Suppose that A.D. 1915 should pass with the world's

affairs all serene and with evidence that the "very elect" had not been "changed" and without the restoration of natural Israel to favor under the New Covenant (Romans 11:12,15). What then? Would not that prove a keen disappointment? Indeed it would! It would work irreparable wreck to the parallel dispensations and Israel's trouble, and to the Jubilee calculations, and to the prophecy of the 2300 days of Daniel, and to the epoch called "Gentile Times," and to the 1,260, 1,290 and 1,335 days....None of these would be available longer....What a blow that would be.[286]

As we will note, the Watchtower Society's eventual response was to either change the dates or to admit human error, but not to admit false prophecy (at least until 1968).

When the 1914 events did not occur, they were rescheduled for 1918–1925. When they did not occur in 1918–1925, the WS again changed or deleted the dates in its literature to cover up the embarrassment.[287] In the 1917 edition of *The Finished Mystery* (claimed to be the posthumous work of Russell and Volume 7 of his *Studies in the Scriptures*),[288] Armageddon was to begin in "the Spring of 1918" (p. 62). There was to be "worldwide all-embracing anarchy" in the "fall of 1920" (p. 542; the 1926 ed. reads "in the end of the time of trouble"). Likewise, the 1917 edition asserts that Revelation 11:13 would be fulfilled "early in 1918" (the "earthquake") and in "the fall of 1920" (the fire, p. 178). The 1926 edition is again altered.[289]

After Russell's death, Rutherford continued and expanded this tradition of false prophecies and covering up failures. He believed that 1925 would mark the year of Christ's Kingdom. He was wrong.[290] The *Watchtower* of September 1, 1922 (p. 262), stated, "The date 1925 is even more distinctly indicated by the Scriptures because it is fixed by the law of God to Israel....[One can see how] even before 1925 the great crisis would be reached and probably passed." The *Watchtower* of April 1, 1923 (page 106), stated, "Our thought is that 1925 is definitely settled by the Scriptures." But what happened when 1925 arrived? The *Watchtower* of January 1, 1925, was less certain: "The year 1925 is here. With great expectation Christians have looked forward to this year. Many have confidently expected that all members of the body of Christ will be changed to heavenly glory during the year. This may be accomplished. It may not be."[291]

What happened near the end of 1925? In the September 1925 *Watchtower,* we find the importance of 1925 being denied: "It is to be expected that Satan will try to inject into the minds of the consecrated the thought that 1925 should see an end of the work, and that therefore it would be needless for them to do more."[292] After all the divinely inspired WS promises for 1925, all of a sudden Satan, not God, becomes the one prophesying. Rutherford noted in 1931,

> There was a measure of disappointment on the part of Jehovah's faithful ones on earth concerning the years 1914, 1918 and 1925, which disappointment lasted for a time. Later the faithful learned that these dates were definitely fixed in the Scriptures [concerning other matters]; and they also learned to quit fixing dates for the future and predicting what would come to pass on certain dates, but to rely (and they do rely) upon the Word of God as to the events that must come to pass.[293]

In light of almost half a century of false prophecies, Jehovah's Witnesses apparently stopped date-setting (at least) for about 40 years, but they continued to hold out the promise of the imminency of Armageddon and the subsequent Kingdom. Again, the Witness looks forward to the Battle of Armageddon in the same manner that the Christian looks forward to the Second Coming of Christ. From 1930 to 1939 there were numerous predictions:

> 1930—The great climax is at hand.[294]

1931—God's Kingdom has begun to operate. His day of vengeance is here and Armageddon is at hand.[295]

1933—The overwhelming testimony of the prophecy and of the supporting facts shows that the cleansing of the sanctuary has been accomplished and this indicates that Armageddon draws nigh.[296]

In a "Testimony to the Rulers of the World," Rutherford stated,

That Satan's lease of power is done, that the old world has ended, and that the time is at hand when Christ Jesus...will oust Satan the [wicked] one and begin His righteous government which will establish God's will on earth....Evil forces are gathering the whole world unto the great battle of the Lord God Almighty; that there is now impending a time of trouble such as the world has never known.[297]

1939—The battle of the great day of God Almighty is very near.[298]

We collected in our files 44 predictions, from May 1940 to April 15, 1943, of the imminence of Armageddon, variously phrased. We list only the briefest data here. All but two are quotations from the *Watchtower*. Some are qualified by "all the facts now indicate," "strongly indicates," "suggests," and such like, but the overall message is undeniable:

May 1940—Armageddon is very near (May 1940, *Informant,* p. 1).

September 1940—The Kingdom is here, the King is enthroned. Armageddon is just ahead....The great climax has been reached (September 1940, *The Messenger,* p. 6).

January 1, 1941—Armageddon is very near (p. 11).

May 15, 1941—The time is short now till the universal war of Armageddon (p. 159).

August 1, 1941—Armageddon, which is near (p. 235).

September 15, 1941—The FINAL END IS VERY NEAR (p. 276; compare p. 287).

October 15, 1941—The battle of Armageddon is quite near (p. 319).

November 1, 1941—Armageddon is very near (p. 325).

January 15, 1942—The time is at hand for Jesus Christ to take possession of all things (p. 28).

February 1, 1942—The time is short (p. 45; compare p. 39).

March 1, 1942—The "end of the world" at Armageddon, now near (p. 74; compare p. 69).

May 1, 1942—Now, with Armageddon immediately before us (p. 139).

May 15, 1942—All such are the sure signs of the FINAL END (p. 157).

June 15, 1942—The glorious day of the triumph of Jehovah's THEOCRACY…is at hand (p. 188).

July 15, 1942—Armageddon, which final battle is very near (p. 224).

August 15, 1942—The impending battle of Armageddon (p. 243; compare p. 253).

April 15, 1943—The impending cataclysm of Armageddon (p. 126).

May 1, 1943—The final end of all things…is at hand (p. 139).

August 15, 1943—The battle of Armageddon cannot be sidetracked; all nations are remorsely marching nearer and nearer to it (p. 252).

September 1, 1944—Armageddon is near at hand (p. 264).

Even after World War II ended, in 1946 we read, "The disaster of Armageddon…is at the door."[299] And the period of 1950 to 1980 is full of "announcements" similar to what we have just quoted. Numerous books and the *Watchtower* have continued what Gruss labels "the illusion of urgency." Several from the 1950s are typical:

1950—The March is on! Where? To the field of Armageddon for the "war of the great day of God the Almighty."[300]

1953—Armageddon is so near at hand it will strike the generation now living.[301] The year 1954 was thought by many Witnesses to be "the Year."[302]

1955—It is becoming clear that the war of Armageddon is near its breaking-out point.[303]

1958—When will Armageddon be fought? Jehovah the great Timekeeper has scheduled Armageddon to come at the close of the "time of the end." That time is near. How near?…No man knows that date, but we do know it will be very soon. How do we know it is soon? Because the time left for the Devil, now that Christ has hurled the Devil down to the earth, is called "a short period of time" (Revelation 12:12). The time left for the Devil's world is now very short.[304]

The long march of the world powers is nearing its end. World-shattering events are just before us. Jehovah's history written in advance makes certain of this to us [sic].[305]

The October 8, 1968, *Awake!* (p. 23), stated that "certain persons" had previously *falsely* predicted the end of the world, and that what they lacked was God's guidance! It even said that "they were guilty of false prophesying." But now, supposedly, this false prophesying is over:

True, there have been those in times past who predicted an "end to the world," even announcing a specific date. Some have gathered groups of people with
them and fled to the hills or withdrawn into their
houses waiting for the end. Yet, nothing happened.
The "end" did not come. *They were guilty of false
prophesying.* Why? What was missing? Missing was
the full measure of evidence required in fulfillment of
Bible prophecy. *Missing from such people were God's
truths and the evidence that he was guiding and using
them.* But what about today? Today we have the evidence required, all of it. And it is overwhelming!
[Emphasis added.]

Here the Watchtower Society actually admits to false prophecy,
explaining it as a lack of God's guidance. But they next claim that
the situation is far different now, because they have all "the evidence" that God is guiding them, and "it is overwhelming." The
stage had been set for the 1975 prophecy of Armageddon. In 1971,
"Shortly within our twentieth century, the 'battle in the day of
Jehovah' will begin against the modern antitype of Jerusalem,
Christendom." (*The Nations Shall Know That I Am Jehovah—
How?* 1971, p. 216); in 1973 we read, "The day when the unparalleled 'great tribulation' breaks upon...Christendom, is very
near....There is no reason for us to be uncertain with regard to the
period of time in which we are living."[306]

Prior to 1975, Jehovah's Witnesses were once again led to
believe in date-setting for the year 1975, in spite of the fact that in
1963 they were told that "it does no good to use Bible chronology
for speculating on dates that are still future."[307] Edmond Gruss'
devastating exposé, *Jehovah's Witnesses and Prophetic Speculation,*
published in 1972, stated: "In the mind of the average Witness
there is little or no doubt that the [1975] date is correct. This
conclusion was drawn by the writer from his conversations with
individual Jehovah's Witnesses. The same impression was
reported by Ruth Brandon in her article, 'Jehovah 1975': 'For the

Witness', there's no question of "if." Armageddon *will* happen in 1975, if not earlier.'"[308]

Why did the WS return to date-setting? Because they had no choice. Their own (again false) chronology demanded it. The Witnesses had taught that Armageddon must precede the 1000-year reign of Christ, and their chronology taught that there was a literal 6000 years of human history prior to this. Thus, when they declared that the 6000 years was to end in 1975, Armageddon had to occur before or in 1975. In the following quote (made in 1966), they stated that the year of the Jubilee would parallel the seventh millennium and begin in 1975:

> God's own written Word indicates it is the appointed time for it [the Jubilee year, that is, the millennium]....
> According to this trustworthy Bible chronology six thousand years from man's creation will end in 1975, and the seventh period of a thousand years of human history will begin in the fall of 1975 C.E....How appropriate it would be for Jehovah God to make of this coming seventh period of a thousand years a sabbath period of rest and release, a great Jubilee sabbath....It would not be by mere chance of accident but would be according to the loving purpose of Jehovah God for the reign of Jesus Christ, the "Lord of the sabbath," to run parallel with the seventh millennium of man's existence....The blessed time for its introduction is fast approaching....The long-awaited time for this is at hand![309]

Thus there can be no doubt that for Jehovah's Witnesses 1975 was to be "the Year." In 1975, as if there were no possibility of failure, the Society states: "The fulfillment...is immediately ahead of us."[310] "Unequaled world distress lies just ahead of us."[311] And that there is "lifesaving work...[which] yet remains to be done before the current world distress reaches its culmination in the 'great tribulation.'"[312] The October 1, 1975, issue (p. 94) referred to "the approaching great tribulation." Despite the additional failure, the *Watchtower* continued its emphasis on Armageddon. The September 22, 1976, issue (p. 31), declared "a global disaster, unparalleled in human history, is very near."

The mid to late 1970s had article titles such as the following, which were emphasized on the front cover of the *Watchtower:*

March 15, 1976—Reconciliation Through God's Mercy Before Har-Magedon

December 15, 1976—Hold on—the Promise Nears Fulfillment

March 1, 1978—Our Incoming World Government—God's Kingdom

June 15, 1979—A Day of Reckoning at Hand

November 1, 1979—Christian Neutrality as God's War Approaches

October 15, 1979—Take Courage the Millennium Is at Hand

Statements from 1980 well into the new millennium have shown no Watchtower repentance in this matter; in fact, they have continued such deceptive practices and false prophecies. For example, in "Armageddon by 2000 A.D. says 'Jehovah,'" Stett and Kotwall provide numerous prophesies from WS literature arguing that Armageddon was to occur by A.D. 2000, for example, "Some of that 'generation' [of 1914] could survive until the end of the century. But there are many indications that 'the end' is much closer than that!" (the *Watchtower,* March 1, 1984, pp. 18–19); "With confidence in the [Revelation 7:9] vision's complete fulfillment during the decades of this 20th century the anointed remnant of the bride class have never let up in saying 'Come!'" (1989 *Yearbook* of Jehovah's Witnesses, p. 3); "Jehovah's prophetic word through Christ Jesus is: 'This generation [of 1914] will by no means pass away until all things occur'(Luke 21:32). And Jehovah, who is the source of inspired and unfailing prophecy, will bring about the fulfillment" (the *Watchtower,* May 15, 1984, pp. 6–7; www.watchtowerinformationservice.org/2000.html).

The official WS website carried the following statements at the time of publication: "How can we know that we are very close to the time when God will bring an end to [the world]? Time is running out for this world." "How thrilling it is to realize that the fulfillment of those glorious prophecies is but a short time off!" ("How We Know We Are in 'the Last Days,' Part 9," www.watch tower.org/library/dg/article_09.htm). "Soon, when God brings this present wicked system of things to its end, Trinitarian Christendom will be called to account. And she will be judged adversely for her God-dishonoring actions and doctrines." ("Worship God on His Terms," <www.watchtower.org/library/ti/article_09.htm>.)

We have now listed a reasonable number of statements showing that the Watchtower Society, since its beginning, has been claiming an imminent end to the world. If the Watchtower Society has been indisputably *wrong* in every era it has been prophesying, how can it possibly be trusted by modern Jehovah's Witnesses? How can their prophetic statements be considered true and to genuinely reflect God's guidance of the Watchtower when they are proved false by the calendar? Calendars have no bias against the WS. Would any employer hire a criminal for the tenth time after nine repeated jailings for offenses against the employer? How can the Society possibly claim to be the "faithful, reliable, trustworthy" servant of God and expect members to trust it?[313] Read these 1975 Watchtower Society statements carefully:

> A new and better world is at hand....There is no room for doubt about this....[Jehovah's Witnesses] unswerving attention to such inspired prophecy has held them true to the right course till now. And now the new day is dawning and the daystar has risen, and their eyes are blessed with seeing the modern-day fulfillment of Bible prophecy.[314]

> Over the endorsement of God's own name the grand
> things to come—soon—stand fully guaranteed in
> prophecies of his indestructible Word.[315]

The same book even claims of Armageddon that "Jehovah has his own *fixed* date for its arrival."[316] Again, how can "Jehovah God" possibly have been guiding the Watchtower Society for over 100 years when He has His "own fixed date for its arrival"? Clearly, either God has changed His mind from generation to generation, or fallible men who have *never* received divine guidance have lied about it and somehow been directing the Watchtower for the last century.

With all due respect, what can one say of Witnesses who know all this and yet continue to believe in the Watchtower Society as God's true prophet? As Proverbs notes, "Wisdom is too high for a fool..." (Proverbs 24:7). Yet Witnesses are the very ones who assert, "Christians holding to true prophecy do not follow...false teachers."[317]

What makes matters worse is that individual Witnesses are pressured to deny the existence of false prophecy because to admit to their existence might lead to the consequences of disfellowship, which makes one worthy of death and eternal annihilation. As Gruss documents, citing court records, a facade of unity is far more important to the Society than any concern with truth.[318] The following brief excerpt is taken from the Pursuer's Proof of a trial held in the Scottish Court of Sessions, November 1954. Microfilm copies are available from The Scottish Records Office, H.M. General Register House, Edinburgh, Scotland. Ask for *The Pursuer's Proof* of Douglas Walsh vs. The Right Honorable James Latham Clyde, M.P., P.C., as representing the Minister of Labour and National Service. The pages in question are numbers 340–43. Haydon C. Covington (who is interviewed here by James Latham Clyde) was the Watchtower's legal counsel and a former vice president:

> Q. Back to the point now. A false prophecy was promulgated?
>
> A. I agree to that.

Q. It had to be accepted by Jehovah's Witnesses?

A. That is correct....

Q. Unity at all costs?

A. Unity at all costs, because we believe and are sure that Jehovah God is using our organization, the governing body of our organization to direct it, even though mistakes are made from time to time.

Q. And unity based upon an enforced acceptance of false prophecy?

A. That is conceded to be true.

Q. And the person who expressed his view, as you say, that it was wrong, and was disfellowshipped, would be in breach of the Covenant, if he was baptized?

A. That is correct.

Q. And as you said yesterday expressly, would be worthy of death?

A. I think—

Q. Would you say yes or no?

A. I will answer yes, unhesitatingly.[319]

24

DOES THE WATCHTOWER SOCIETY NOW ADMIT TO FALSE PROPHECY?

Despite its continuous claims to divine guidance, the WS now admits various failures; it could do little else given all the advance publication for prophecies in 1874, 1914, 1925, and 1975. As we saw, even Rutherford, in his book *Vindication*, confessed, "There was a measurement of disappointment on the part of Jehovah's faithful ones on earth concerning the years 1914, 1918 and 1925...."[320]

Any member who knows that the WS has publicly confessed to false prophecies should immediately recognize that the Society is not guided by God and leave. Nowhere in the Bible do we find God claiming that a prophet might misinterpret Him or that His prophecies may not accurately be received. Nowhere in the Bible do we find a prophet of God having to explain why his prophecies failed. In the following material, we will document that the WS has admitted its errors.

In *Man's Salvation* (1975) the WS admits that Russell was wrong in his 1874 prediction of Christ's Second Coming.[321]

According to *Studies in the Scriptures*,[322] Russell claimed "Our Lord, the appointed King, is now present, since October 1874, A.D."

The WS admitted that it was wrong in the 1914 prediction.

The Grieshabers quote the Watchtower publication *Light* (Book 1), undated (p. 194), as confessing that they were wrong for 40 years in their 1914 prophecy:

> The Watch Tower, and its companion publications of the Society, for forty years emphasized the fact that 1914 would witness the establishment of God's kingdom and the complete glorification of the church....All of the Lord's people looked forward to 1914 with joyful expectation. When that time came and passed there was much disappointment, chagrin and mourning, and the Lord's people were greatly in reproach. They were ridiculed by the clergy and their allies in particular, and pointed to with scorn, because they had said so much about 1914, and what would

come to pass, and their "prophecies" had not been fulfilled.[323]

True, the Bible students were not "taken home" to heaven in October 1914. But the 2,520-year-long Gentile Times then ended.[324]

The WS admitted that it was wrong in 1925.

As the start of the new millennium, 1925 was to mark the resurrection of the prophets of old for ruling in the millennial age. "Therefore we may confidently expect that 1925 will mark the return of Abraham, Isaac, Jacob and the faithful prophets of old."[325] Yet the 1975 Witness *Yearbook* confesses that it was, in effect, wrong in the 1925 prophecy, also rationalizing its failure:

> Jehovah certainly blessed his people back in the 1920s and provided the things they needed to advance the interests of the Kingdom. He also proved himself to be a God of progressive revelation. The Bible Students, in turn, found it necessary to adjust their thinking to some extent....God's people had to adjust their thinking about 1925, for instance... 1925 was a sad year for many brothers. Some of them were stumbled; their hopes were dashed. They had hoped to see some of the "ancient worthies" [men of old like Abraham] resurrected. Instead of its being considered a "probability," they read into it that it was a "certainty" and some prepared for their own loved ones with expectancy of their resurrection.[326]

Does the earlier quote stating "we may confidently expect" 1925 to be "the year" sound like a "probability"?

The 1980 *Yearbook* (pp. 30–31) declares of 1925: "The brothers also appreciated the candor of this same talk, which acknowledged the Society's responsibility for some of the disappointment a number felt regarding 1925." Gruss, in *Apostles of Denial* (p. 26), and others have given further data concerning the certainty of the

1925 date. As we saw, the WS also admitted to false prophecy in the October 8, 1968, *Awake!* magazine. And they admitted that they were wrong in 1975. In what must be one of the great understatements of the twentieth century, the Society's 1975 *Yearbook* explains: "If for any reason the Lord has permitted us to miscalculate the prophecies, the signs of the times assure us that the miscalculations cannot be very great....Jehovah certainly had not forsaken his people or allowed them to be misled."[327] Unbelievably, the same text asserts that "Jehovah's servants" for over 100 years "enjoyed spiritual enlightenment and divine direction" (p. 245).

Did they? Has the Watchtower Society passed the second "test" of having their prophecies "come to pass"? Since biblical standards are the admitted WS standard for judging prophetic accuracy, we can but cite it once more. The prophet is "recognized as one truly sent by the LORD *only* if his prediction comes true" (Jeremiah 28:9, emphasis added).

25

Has the Watchtower Society Made Important Changes in Its Divine Revelations?

A third test for WS claims concerns the immutability of divine revelation. An immutable God who faithfully guides the Watchtower Society would, by definition, not repeatedly change His mind on numerous important issues.

Granted, the Jehovah's Witnesses teaching on progressive revelation does allow for new information to be brought to light. However, biblically, progressive revelation never contradicts, denies, or changes earlier revelation. Yet this is exactly what we find in the Watchtower, and it raises the question: How can a God who repeatedly changes His mind be trusted? Further, if the Watchtower has changed its mind before, how do we know that what members have complete faith in today will not be changed by the WS tomorrow? Indeed, a number of former Witnesses have cited this quandary as one reason for their leaving the organization. Gruss recounts one incident and then comments on it:

> A short time later the Society changed the meaning of a Bible passage for the second time (Romans 13:1,2). This was the final straw!…It was then that I started searching through the back issues of *The Watchtower.* I found many more discrepancies, contradictions, and changes of interpretation.[328]

> Considering the changes in doctrinal matters and the errors in prophetic speculation over the years, it is difficult, if not impossible, to believe that this organization is the sole recipient of, or is guided at all by, God's Holy Spirit.[329]

How big is the problem? Gruss asserts that "*thousands* of reinterpretations of Scripture and many new doctrinal points have evolved since Russell's death," and he provides a number of examples in his book.[330] Van Baalen observes that W.J. Schnell reports, "As a progressive light worshipper and Jehovah's Witness in good standing, I had observed the *Watchtower* magazine change our doctrines between 1917 and 1928, no less than 148 times."[331] An example can be seen at Luke 16:19-31, where Jesus discusses the reality of hell. This has been interpreted by the Society in at least five different ways. These are not minor changes but major reinterpretations.[332] These changes took place in:

1908 during the Russell-White debate

1928 in Rutherford's *Reconciliation* (pp. 175–76)

1942 in *The New World* (pp. 360–61)

1946 in *Let God Be True* (1st ed., p. 79)

1952 in *Let God Be True* (revised, p. 98)

The WS claims that God has always guided WS leadership to give its people the true interpretation of the Bible "in due time."

How does God change His mind so easily on thousands of occasions? If the dismal record of the WS is our guide, how is it possible to know what the true interpretation of *any* biblical passage is?

Another example is their history text, *Jehovah's Witnesses in the Divine Purpose* (1959), which "rewrites the history and the facts in many places, and authority for almost every statement is from Watchtower sources. Many views held in the early years of the movement are either reinterpreted or not mentioned....This history is full of inaccuracies...."[333] Gruss provides 17 examples of rewriting the facts, distortions, biased reporting, and unjustified changes in the Watchtower Society's own history and doctrines.[334] All this was done under "God's guidance and direction"! Gruss concludes: "The speculations which have been presented are only a small example of what can be found in a limited area. It should be remembered that this speculation was presented with definiteness, as reasonable and as Scriptural."[335]

The faithful and wise servant

A crucial example of change in WS doctrine involves the "faithful and wise servant" in Matthew 24:45. The average Jehovah's Witness today believes that the "faithful and wise servant" refers to a servant class of people, the "144,000 elect," particularly the ones living at Watchtower headquarters in Bethel, who dispense the true food of God (properly interpreting His Word and will) to over 10 million Jehovah's Witnesses. Truth comes from God only by means of "the faithful and wise servant," now believed to be this class of people.[336] Yet the Watchtower Society claims that C.T. Russell never claimed to be "that servant." "From this it is clearly seen that the editor and publisher of *Zion's Watch Tower* disavowed any claim to being individually, in his person, that 'faithful and wise servant.' He never did claim to be such."[337]

True, as a young man Russell claimed that he was not that servant, but under "divine guidance" he later changed his mind and taught he was that servant. Now, if God's truth is said to come *only* from this servant, if it were Russell, then God's channel was permanently terminated with his death because Russell never changed his mind about his status or appointed a successor. Further, because the WS has altered or denied so many of Russell's earlier "divinely guided" teachings, the Society must be guilty of altering God's personal revelation of His will for His people.

When Judge Rutherford entered the picture, he had his own ideas besides those of Russell. He changed Russell's teaching to apply the "faithful and wise servant" to a group of people, to those whom he headed, presumably to justify his own divine authority and guidance. This new teaching ("that servant" being a class of people rather than a person, Russell) caused a serious rift in the membership: Numerous splinter groups arose who claimed allegiance (and still do) to Russell alone as God's channel of truth. Today, the Layman's Home Missionary Movement strongly opposes the Watchtower Society where it has altered Russell's teachings; it believes Russell to be "the servant" of Matthew 24. This movement was begun by Paul Johnson, who, believing himself to be Russell's successor, wrote the 17-volume *Epiphany Studies in the Scriptures.* In Volume 4, *Merariism:*

> Johnson...gives numerous additional examples of changes in doctrine and interpretation. He lists 140 contradictions where Rutherford violates Russell's teaching on pages 373–376, and then comments: "If we would point out the details coming under point (62) above—'Misrepresenting thousands of verses properly interpreted by "that Servant" [Russell]'— our list would swell into thousands of details; for almost never does he allude to or quote a passage in an article on his pet views but he corrupts its sense" (p. 377).[338]

The Dawn Bible Students Association is a similar group that originated as Rutherford began to alter Russell's teachings. (Jehovah's Witnesses splinter groups generally have the same basic doctrine because all are essentially Russellite. The division is over the changes instituted by Rutherford.)[339]

If Russell was "that servant," such a role ended with his death, and the Watchtower Society pronouncements from the beginning that contradict him are merely those of deceived men without divine guidance. If Russell was not "that servant," he was in grave error concerning his own divine mission and unlikely to be trustworthy on other matters. Either way, the WS loses. Rival sects, of course, argue that the data strongly affirms that divine revelation ended with Russell. "If Pastor Russell were 'that servant,' then his death would stop all subsequent revelations and the Society's publications would only be a rehash of what Russell taught. So with the establishing of 'the faithful and wise servant' as a class, the Society has left the door open to create or abolish doctrine and policy at will, and without question!"[340]

What did Russell himself teach? The rival sects are correct here. Russell, as early as 1896, wrote that "that servant" was an individual and that he was "that servant."[341] The *Watchtower* of December 1, 1916 (pp. 356–57; reprints, p. 5998), agreed: "Thousands of the readers of Pastor Russell's writings believe that he filled the office of 'that faithful and wise servant,' and that his great work was giving to the household of faith meat in due season [proper Bible interpretation]. His modesty and humility precluded him from openly claiming this title, but he admitted as much in private conversation."[342]

Even Rutherford admitted in the *Watchtower* (March 1, 1917, p. 67): "The Watchtower unhesitatingly proclaims Brother Russell as 'that faithful and wise servant.'" The *Watchtower* (December 15, 1916; Reprints, p. 6024) stated of Russell (for example, his *Studies in the Scriptures*), "To disregard the message would mean to disregard the Lord." The *Watchtower* (December 15, 1918, p. 396) also stated the belief in Russell as "that servant": "This we most certainly hold, both as a fact and as a necessity of faith." Duane Magnani's study, *Who Is the Faithful and Wise Servant?* from which this material was taken, concludes: "Russell never believed another person held this special position of 'That Servant.' Neither did he rebuke his followers for referring to him as this Servant. The record plainly shows that Charles Taze Russell BELIEVED AND TAUGHT that he alone was the Faithful and Wise Servant.... [Yet] the present day Society rejects his claims of spiritual authority."[343]

Thus, one reason the modern Watchtower Society rejects many of Russell's teachings is because his claims, having divine sanction, *deny their own authority.* Yet without Russell's authority, they would not even exist. The WS alteration has been so complete that ordinary Jehovah's Witnesses today will even deny that they are Russellites.[344] Not surprisingly, the Watchtower Society does not sell Russell's *Studies in the Scriptures,* and has not for many years; they can be purchased only from Russellite sects.

But there could be another reason for the WS to de-emphasize Russell. As a false prophet who lied under oath and was unqualified as a Bible teacher, he was one more embarrassment. All this and more is public record concerning Russell.[345] This may explain why Rutherford apparently attempted a "theocratic coup," wherein Russell and the problems associated with him could be eliminated and Rutherford himself could start fresh as "God's new channel." Thus, Rutherford changed a number of things. He instituted the name "Jehovah's Witnesses"—a reflection of his shifting the emphasis from Russell's theology on Christ's atonement to the vindication of Jehovah's name. Rutherford may have felt that Russell had not sufficiently vindicated Jehovah's name. Rutherford also claimed that only with him was divine light now being shed upon certain books. His characteristic approach is typified when in 1931 he said of Ezekiel: "During the centuries that prophecy has been a mystery sealed to all who have sought to unlock it. God's due time has come for the prophecy to be understood."[346] Likewise he said that Daniel could not be understood until post-1918, when it was "revealed" that the League of Nations was the abomination of desolation.[347] Russell, however, had already written some 200 pages on Ezekiel in *The Finished Mystery* (1917). This was now discarded because it did not fit the new teachings of the Watch-tower Society; that is, Rutherford's interpretations. Of course, Rutherford could not dispense with Russell entirely, for he was still the founder and head of the Society.

According to Gruss, Rutherford, in his 1929 book, *Prophecy,* began a dual-era interpretation of Watchtower history based on the Elijah-Elisha partnership in the Old Testament. Russell was Elijah, Rutherford was Elisha. The "Elijah era" was that time wherein God was restoring basic truths to his people (through Russell). This ended in 1918, only two years after Russell's death. The "Elisha era" began in 1919, the year Rutherford was released from prison* and began reorganization of the society. Rutherford, like Elisha, had a "double portion" of the Spirit. He would continue and complete the work "Elijah" had begun, and so he moved quickly to purge his opposition and consolidate his power.[348] During this era some 40,000 of the faithful left the movement.[349] Again, these individuals became the source of the splinter Russellite groups already mentioned.

Russell's prophetic revelation dealt with the 1874 to 1914 era, and his claims did not come to pass. Rutherford "saved the day" by reinterpreting the Scriptures to apply them to his post-1918 era, although in the end he failed just as miserably as Russell. Nevertheless, the idea that new revelation was being given, bringing "new light" upon the Scriptures, was sufficient to satisfy many and to solidify the movement. Under Rutherford's leadership the Society greatly expanded. Major changes were made in Russell's teachings, in effect denying all possibility to Russell's divine inspiration. Thus Russell is largely ignored today by the very organization he founded.

---

* He and other Watchtower Society staff were jailed in accordance with the Antiespionage Act due to their pacifist, anti-Government philosophy.

The WS and Bible interpretation

Although there are thousands of changes in divine revelation, only a few illustrations are needed.* The purpose of this brief section is to document that the average Jehovah's Witness has no basis for trusting the WS claim to properly interpret the Bible under divine guidance.[350]

Abaddon, Apollyon—from Satan to Jesus Christ

This concerns Revelation 9:11 and the identification of the angel of the bottomless pit:

> Original doctrine: "The prince of the power of the air." Ephesians 2:2....That is, Destroyer. But in plain English his name is Satan, the Devil.[351]

> Changed doctrine: "In Hebrew his name is Abaddon, meaning 'Destruction'; and in the Greek it is Apollyon, meaning 'Destroyer.' All this plainly identifies the 'angel' as picturing Jesus Christ, the Son of Jehovah God."[352]

Adam—from resurrection to no resurrection

> Original doctrine: "Just when Adam will be awakened, only the Lord knows. It may be early or it may be late during the period of restoration."[353]

> Changed doctrine: "There is no promise found in the Scriptures that Adam's redemption and resurrection and salvation will take place at any time. Adam had a fair trial for life and completely failed."[354] In recent writings, Adam and Eve were viewed as among those who are incorrigible sinners who "proved that they were not worthy of life, and they will not be resurrected."[355]

---

*These are excerpted for convenient reference, and used with permission, from Gruss' *We Left Jehovah's Witnesses: A Non-Prophet Organization*, pp. 156-59.

Sodom and Gomorrah—resurrection promised, resurrection denied, resurrection reinstated

Original doctrine: "Thus our Lord teaches that the Sodomites did not have a full opportunity; and he guarantees them such opportunity."[356]

Changed doctrine: "He was pinpointing the utter impossibility of ransom for unbelievers or those willfully wicked, because Sodom and Gomorrah were irrevocably condemned and destroyed, beyond any possible recovery."[357]

Return to former position: "As in the case of Tyre and Sidon, Jesus showed that Sodom, bad as it was, had not got to the state of being unable to repent....So the spiritual recovery of the dead people of Sodom is not hopeless."[358]

Worship of Jesus Christ—from acceptance to rejection

Original doctrine: "*Question....*Was he *really* worshiped or is the translation faulty? *Answer.* Yes, we believe our Lord while on earth was really worshiped, and properly so....It was proper for our Lord to receive worship."[359] "He was the object of unreproved worship even when a babe, by the wise men who came to see the new-born king....He never reproved any for acts of worship offered to Himself....Had Christ not been *more* than man the same reason would have prevented Him from receiving worship."[360] "The purposes of this Society are:...public Christian worship of Almighty God and Jesus Christ; to arrange for and hold local and world-wide assemblies for such worship."[361]

Changed doctrine: "No distinct worship is to be rendered to Jesus Christ now glorified in heaven. Our worship is to go to Jehovah God."[362] "For example, the magi from the east and King Herod said they wanted to 'do obeisance to' (*proskyneo*) the babe that had been born King of the Jews. 'Do obeisance' is preferable here because neither the magi nor King Herod meant to worship the babe as God." [363]

Resurrection from the dead—from all to some

Original doctrine: "All are to be awakened from the Adamic death, as though from a sleep, by virtue of the ransom given." [364] "Under this new covenant the whole human race shall have the opportunity to come back to God through Jesus Christ the mediator." [365]

Changed doctrine: "It has been held by many that the Scriptures guarantee that 'all must come back from the dead' at Christ's return and during his thousand-year rule." [366] "That conclusion does not appear to have support in reason or in the Scriptures." [367]

Israel—physical Israel to spiritual Israel

Original doctrine: "That the re-establishment of Israel in the land of Palestine is one of the events to be expected in this Day of the Lord, we are fully assured by the above expression of the Prophet [commenting on Amos 9:11, 14-15]. Notice, particularly, that the prophecy cannot be interpreted in any symbolic sense." [368] "The promise, time and again repeated, that the Lord would regather them and bless them in the land and *keep them there* and bless them forever is conclusive proof that, the promise must be fulfilled....Behold, that time is now at hand!" [369] (See also Rutherford's *Life*.)

Changed doctrine: "Nothing in the modern return of Jews to Palestine and the setting up of the Israeli republic corresponds with the Bible prophecies concerning the restoration of Jehovah's name-people to his favor and organization....The remnant of spiritual Israelites, as Jehovah's Witnesses, have proclaimed world-wide the establishment of God's kingdom in 1914."[370]

The "superior authorities" of Romans 13—from earthly rulers, to Jehovah and Jesus, to earthly rulers

Original doctrine: Until 1929 it was taught that the "higher powers" or "superior authorities" (*New World Translation*) were the earthly rulers to whom the Christian paid taxes, etc.[371]

Changed doctrine: From 1929 to 1962 the "superior authorities" were explained as "the Most High God Jehovah and his exalted Son Jesus Christ."[372]

Return to former position: "In spite of the end of the Gentile Times in 1914, God permitted the political authorities of this world to continue as the 'higher powers' or the 'powers that be,' which are 'ordained of God.' "[373]

The great crowd ("other sheep," the non-144,000 Jehovah's Witnesses) as a spiritual class—yes, no

Original doctrine: "*Does the Great Company receive life direct from God on the spirit plane?* Answer—Yes, they receive life direct in that they have been begotten of the Holy Spirit, and when they are begotten they are just the same way as the little flock, because we are called in the one hope of our calling. They do not make their calling and election sure, but not being worthy of second death, they therefore receive life on the spirit plane."[374] "Ever and anon someone advances the conclusion that the 'great multitude' will not be a spiritual class. The prophecy of Ezekiel shows that such conclusion is erroneous. The fact that their position is seven steps higher than the outside shows that they must be made spirit creatures....They must be spirit creatures in order to be in the outer court of the divine structure, described by Ezekiel."[375]

Changed doctrine: "Thus the great multitude is definitely identified, not as a spirit-begotten class whose hopes are for a place in heaven, but a class trusting in the Lord, and who hope for everlasting life on earth."[376]

Do the previous examples support the claim that the Watchtower Bible and Tract Society "from the time of its organization until now" has been God's "sole collective channel for the flow of Biblical truth to men on earth"? Do the examples support the claim that all Witness interpretations emanate from God? Or do they prove that the interpretations merely originate from the minds of confused or corrupt men? Indeed, at this point, one can only agree with the Watchtower Society: "Jehovah never makes any mistakes. Where the student relies upon man, he is certain to be led into difficulties."[377] "Men not only contradict God, they contradict one another. How can they be reliable guides—unless their words are based on God's words? But how can you know whether they are or not? By going directly to God's Word as your source of authority. Search for yourself and let God be true!"[378]

Not surprisingly, many former Jehovah's Witnesses will testify to leaving the Watchtower Society because of "going directly to God's Word" as their source of authority and spiritual enlightenment. More than one Witness has broken ranks with the WS after taking to heart signs at rallies protesting the WS that say "Read the Bible, not the Watchtower."

In conclusion, the Watchtower Society has not passed this test concerning the veracity of divine revelation because it has changed its own divine revelations in countless places.

26

CAN THE WATCHTOWER SOCIETY CLAIM DIVINE GUIDANCE AND AUTHORITY WHEN IT MISUSES QUOTED SOURCES?

It is obvious that the true God, who is himself "the God of truth" and who hates lies, will not look with favor on persons who cling to organizations that teach falsehood (Psalm 31:5; Proverbs 6:16-19; Revelation 21:8). And, really, would you want to be even associated with a religion that had not been honest with you? (*Is This Life All There Is?*, 1974, p. 46.)

A fourth and final test concerns care and accuracy in quoting other sources and authors. Watchtower defenders of their beliefs often appeal to Greek grammars or lexicons, Bible dictionaries and encyclopedias, and other authoritative sources, and they seem quite convincing to someone who reads them and assumes the integrity of the Society. However, as with Mormonism, a cardinal rule when studying Watchtower literature is always to read the quoted sources in their original context, because the original will often be misquoted. Many researchers have noted this tendency. In his detailed study, Gruss discovered: "This writer has found that in many cases the Watchtower publications have either misrepresented or misunderstood the sources they have utilized."[379] In *The Scholastic Dishonesty of the Watchtower,* Van Buskirk agreed: "In reviewing the above subjects one finds that the Watchtower Bible and Tract Society thinks nothing of misquoting and misrepresenting historians....Several Greek scholars are quoted completely out of context....There is no hesitancy to twist and to lie outright about the earlier doctrines held by their own founders."[380] In addition, the Watchtower Society also employs the writings of liberal theologians and agnostics—virtually anyone they can squeeze doctrinal support from.[381]

Indeed, the duplicity is sufficiently evident that one could almost expect misquoting *whenever* the WS is seeking to establish unbiblical doctrines from sources generally considered scholarly, reliable, and/or evangelical, simply because the WS theology can only document false teachings by misquoting reliable sources which deal honestly with the data of history, historical theology, systematic theology, biblical languages, and so on.

Among the sources misquoted are the following: McClintock and Strong's *Cyclopaedia of Biblical Theological and Ecclesiastical*

Literature (1871);[382] Alexander Hislop's *The Two Babylons*;[383] Edwin R. Thiele's *The Mysterious Numbers of the Hebrew Kings*;[384-385] Robertson's *A Grammar of the Greek New Testament*;[386] Westcott and Hort's Greek text;[387] William Barclay's *Many Witnesses, One Lord*;[388-390] the *New International Dictionary of New Testament Theology*;[391-392] Dana and Mantey's *Manual Grammar of the Greek New Testament*;[393-395] *The Encyclopedia Britannica, The New Catholic Encyclopedia, The Encyclopedia Americana*;[396] and various commentators on the NWT (see www.freeminds.org/doctrine/nwt.htm).

The Watchtower Society has now thoroughly failed four tests of its claim to be God's sole channel for accurately disseminating the true interpretation of God's word and will. First, it has failed accuracy of biblical translation by deliberately mistranslating the Bible in hundreds or thousands of places. Second, it has failed accuracy in prophecy by declaring hundreds of false prophecies as God's truth. Third, it has failed in the area of divine revelation because its own revelations have been changed in countless places. And fourth, it has failed accuracy in reporting of history, doctrine, interpretation, and source documentation by changing or misrepresenting thousands of things. Why then should the WS be taken seriously by anyone?

27

WHAT ARE SOME ETHICAL CONCERNS WITH THE WATCHTOWER SOCIETY?

According to other researchers and former members, Watchtower Society leaders have apparently been involved in shady financial activities, racism, vulgar language at Bethel, fraudulent schemes, cruelty, false advertising, lies, perjury, and bribery, much of this being documented by court records.[397] The late Dr. Walter Martin referred to "proof of their founder's inherent dishonesty and lack of morals."[398] Evidently the lives of both Russell and

Rutherford[399] were not shining examples of Christian character, and the legacy has, variously, continued to the present. Books by Raymond Franz, *Crisis of Conscience* (400 pages) and *In Search of Christian Freedom* (700 pages), have further substantiated some of these charges. In 2002, there was the possibility of a looming pedophilia sex scandal. (Compare Peter Smith, *Courier-Journal* [Louisville, KY], February 4, 2001 <www.courier-journal.com>; <www.silentlambs.org>; *Newsweek,* June 24, 2002; *New York Post,* May 9, 2002.)

The WS position on blood transfusions, wherein thousands have needlessly lost their lives,[400] is clearly a moral issue and one we will comment on. Of course, so is WS deception in Bible translation, prophecy, and other areas, which has brought grief or ruin to thousands more. What of the many Witnesses, who, believing the end of the world was imminent, sold homes, quit jobs, and made financial decisions that reduced them to poverty? According to former members, it appears that irresponsibility, "callousness and indifference [are] often shown by the Watchtower Society hierarchy" in situations like this or when WS interests are at stake.[401] There is also the unconscionable fact that the WS has not taken responsibility for any of this.

Below we briefly consider the Society's blood transfusion policy, religious hatred and potential violence, and mental illness concerns.

Blood transfusion policy deaths

No one knows how many Witnesses have voluntarily taken their own lives or sacrificed the lives of their children due to the Watchtower Society's ban on blood transfusions (which began only in 1961), but the number is at least in the tens of thousands. David A. Reed's *Blood on the Altar: Confessions of a Jehovah's Witness Minister* (Prometheus, 1996) offers details, pointing out that thousands of Witnesses have literally bled to death in obedience to the Watchtower. Reed estimates almost 9000 die each year. He offers medical statistics and case histories that include names, dates, attending physicians, and hospitals.

As in Christian Science (for different reasons), a Witness will actually allow himself or his own children to die rather than permit a medical solution if it involves a blood transfusion. Witnesses have even sued doctors for saving their lives! Because transfusions are allegedly a violation of God's "law," and can result in *eternal* death (annihilation), the reasoning is that it is better to die physically and at least have the hope of re-creation. As one faithful Witness declared, "I would rather see my boy dead and in the grave than see him violate Jehovah God's commandment against blood." In this sad case, as so often happens, she received her wish and saw her own son placed into the grave.[402]

In defending this doctrine, the Watchtower Society utilizes Genesis 9:4, Leviticus 17:14, and other biblical passages as proof texts. The above Scriptures only prohibit the eating of blood, which has nothing to do with transfusion for medical purposes. In addition, they refer to animal blood in Old Testament sacrifices, not human blood. The reason for the prohibition is given in Leviticus 17:11: the blood of animals partaking in sacrifice was sacred, and because "the life of a creature is in the blood" it must be respected, not eaten. Genesis 9:4 also refers to the eating of animal blood, a not infrequent pagan practice done in the assumption that one is transferring the animal's life force into oneself for power. In Acts 15:20,29, abstaining "from blood" also refers to animal blood and has nothing to do with transfusions or eternal death. Not one biblical verse anywhere prohibits blood transfusions.

Blood transfusion involves the saving of life. Even orthodox Jews who hold to strict Old Testament laws, and who certainly know how to translate the Old Testament more accurately than the WS, accept the practice of blood transfusion. The Watchtower Society ban is simply a result of the irresponsibility of biblically ignorant people. Even if eating blood meant transfusion, in his *Jehovah's Witnesses and Blood Transfusion* Dr. Havor Montague shows that under Jewish law such transfusion would have been permitted in order to save a life, because to save a life is more important than to not eat blood.[403] His analysis refutes a number of other Watchtower Society positions on this issue.

Similarly, at the probable cost of many lives and much misery, the Watchtower Society also once denied immunizations as being "against the law of God," but years later changed its mind. For many years the Society also denied organ transplants, which it now accepts.

> What is the significance of this vaccination position held by the Society until 1952? Thousands of Witness parents and children were placed in the position of keeping "God's law" (the erroneous Watchtower dictum) and lying to school authorities. Men were needlessly in solitary confinement because of the error of the Society. Why did the official position of the Society not change until 1952? Will a discovery of erroneous teaching also be found in the Society's ban on blood transfusions? The problem on this point is that thousands will have already sacrificed their lives on the altar of Watchtower error.[404]

Indeed, there have been various reports (for example, the *Watchtower*, June 15, 2000) that suggest a change in doctrine may be underway, despite the official WS website retaining the statement in late 2002 that members "refuse to accept blood" transfusions (www.watchtower.org/library/hb/index.htm). The WS may have, incrementally, begun to lift its ban, with the current teaching that certain unique blood products may be used in some cases. While full revision may eventually occur, so many lives have already been lost defending the practice that it would be difficult for the Society to admit its error. We might expect that before needed change arrives, thousands more lives could be callously and needlessly discarded:

> Extensive research will reveal that the arguments presented here cannot be answered by the Watchtower

with its invalid positions. Extensive communication with prominent members of the Society has not produced any satisfactory answers to the question against the blood issue put forth here....Neither the Society nor its publications can justify the deaths of faithful Witnesses on the basis that the Society tries to present as Biblical evidence.[405]

When and if the official policy is changed, one wonders who will pay for the perhaps 50-100,000 dead whose lives have been sacrificed needlessly to WS dogma. That is a great weight to bear, indeed.

Religious hatred and violence

Prior to this edition, we had not particularly considered the WS as a "hate" organization. But clearly of concern today is religiously induced hatred or violence where, for example, something like the Koran can logically be used for either good or evil, depending on the divine commands selected, and the accompanying interpretation of Muslim clerics. And, directly or indirectly, we also find this harmful potential in many of the new religions as well, from certain Eastern and occult sects to more "traditional" groups, including, apparently, the Jehovah's Witnesses.

In the latter case, in addition to the authoritarianism, isolationist tendencies, and an "us vs. them" attitude, there may be an overemphasis upon the "righteous" hatred of those who are seen as "enemies" of Jehovah. For example,

"Haters of God and His people...are to be hated.... We must hate in the truest sense, which is to regard with extreme and active aversion, to consider as loathsome, odious, filthy, to detest. Surely any haters of God are not fit to live on this beautiful earth. The earth will be rid of the wicked and we shall not need to cause physical harm to come to them, for God will attend to that, but we must have a proper perspective of these enemies....We pray with intensity...and plead that His

anger be made manifest....O Jehovah God of hosts...
Be not merciful to any wicked transgressors....Con-
sume them in wrath, consume them so that they shall
be no more." (The *Watchtower*, October 1, 1952, pp.
596-604, from Martin, *Jehovah of the Watchtower*, p.
109.)

Somehow, the always powerful biblical message of God's love
and mercy (for example, John 3:16) and the teaching of Jesus to
love one's enemies has been lost. If such religious hatred is
encouraged in a world where secular "values" have no logical basis
to counter it, the outcome may become part of that "iceberg
beneath the surface" phenomena found in harmful cults that is
recognized too infrequently. For example, the book *Blood Crimes*
recalls how Jehovah's Witnesses' teenagers—17-year-old Bryan
Freeman, 15-year-old brother David, and cousin Ben Birdwell—
"slit their father's throat, stabbed their mother numerous times,
and murdered their brother Eric with a baseball bat." Raised
Jehovah's Witnesses, they had nevertheless become "skinheads"
who hated minorities. So why did they murder their parents and
brother, and what's the connection to Jehovah's Witnesses? To be
sure, many elements entered into the murders, but it appears clear
that WS teachings played an important role.

> What at first seems like 180° conversion in values is
> actually shown to be a refocusing of the hatred taught
> by the Watchtower. Both the Jehovah's Witnesses and
> the skinheads are hate groups; only the focus of their
> hate and how their hate is acted out varies. Research
> on the Jehovah's Witnesses in the concentration
> camps during World War II reveals one of the reasons
> why Witnesses and Nazis batted heads so often was
> because they were in many ways much alike—both
> were highly authoritarian groups convinced only they
> had the truth and the answers to the world's prob-
> lems. They both also taught that opposers should be
> eliminated, the Nazis by the inevitable rule of history

and the Witnesses by Jehovah God. Fred Rosen skillfully shows the important influence of Watchtower teaching in the murder of the boys' parents and brother. The book also eloquently documents not only the failure of the Watchtower, but also the failure of secular social service agencies....This is not the first case of Witness patricide—this writer is aware of many others involving Witnesses—nor will it be the last case. (Jerry Bergman's July 1998 review of Fred Rosen, *Blood Crimes: the Pennsylvania Skinhead Murders* [1996] <www.watchtowerinformationservice .org/bloodcrimes.htm>.)

The author of the above book review is Dr. Jerry Bergman. Dr. Bergman holds a Ph.D. in human biology from Columbia Pacific University, a Ph.D. in evaluation and research from Wayne State University, and is working on a third Ph.D. in molecular biology. He has been a consultant for over 20 science textbooks, presented over 100 scientific papers at professional and community meetings, authored or coauthored over 40 books, monographs, and book chapters, and published over 400 articles in professional journals and popular publications. He has also served as a consultant for ABC News, CBS News, *Reader's Digest,* Amnesty International, several government agencies, and two Nobel Prize winners, as well as testified as an expert witness or consultant in some one hundred court cases.

In his article of several years back, "Growing Up in the Religion of Hate," he recalls his former life in the WS, and offers an eye-opening testimony. Below we site some of his observations:

When I looked into other religious sects—some quite intently...I was able to find no other organization that exercised such an incredibly complete totalitarian autocratic thought control on their members....What do I think about the Watchtower and their doctrine today? My feelings are quite in contrast to what they were only a few years ago. I feel that they are a harmful, hateful organization and do an enormous amount of damage in society.... In the most recent article on how and who to hate, the October 1, 1993, *Watchtower* (p. 19), states that "true Christians...are not curious about apostate ideas. On the contrary, they 'feel a loathing' towards those who have" left or ones who are critical of some aspect of Watchtower policy. One is not to criticize the Watchtower or one is liable to be labeled an apostate. The Watchtower concludes their cacophony of hate and fear by cautioning Witnesses to "leave it to Jehovah to execute vengeance," a comment likely motivated by the death threats and vicious hatred expressed by Witnesses against those who have left. The Watchtower realizes that if their members are caught maiming, or burning the houses or destroying the property of ex-Witnesses, this may reflect poorly upon the Watchtower Society. One would not be surprised that this happens in that the Society teaches "a Christian must hate" those who are critical of the Watchtower.

Having been involved in about 100 litigation cases typically involving a Witness and a non-Witness where custody or alimony was at issue, I came to realize the enormous amount of harm that the Witness teaching of hate produces. Conflicts are normally acerbated in a divorce, but the pure hate that came from the Watchtower followers was blatant and vicious. The Scriptures teach that one should love one's enemies—and these people were not enemies, many were not even Witnesses. They just could not stomach the Watchtower and thus would be considered Watchtower enemies....In my family, the Watchtower caused the divorce of my own parents, many cousins, my own divorce, and the divorces of many of those that I grew up with. Indeed, it has become more and more apparent that the Watchtower leaders are actually "apostles of hate." No small number of Watchtower articles have pushed the need to hate all those that are critical of the Watchtower or do not accept every edict the Watchtower hands down.... The harm is sometimes so severe that suicide, homicide, or even mass murder can result. The horror stories and mental anguish of people involved in the Watchtower because of this hate abounds, as I have documented in my book *Jehovah's Witnesses and the Problem of Mental Health* (Clayton, CA: Witnesses, Inc., 1990).... Probably one of my most devastating experiences involved testifying in American courts on the Watchtower. It was this probably more than any other single experience that caused me to shift my position from neutrality to recognizing the absolute harm that this organization causes in the lives of people.... The modern Watchtower has produced an enormous amount of suffering, far more than under Russell. It has directly caused the loss of tens of thousands of lives because of condemning organ transplants, vaccines, blood transfusions and their inhumane policies such as telling the Witnesses in Malawi they would lose their eternal life if they bought a twenty-five cent party card regardless of the consequences (see Reed, *Worse Than Waco*). While I do not condone the Malawi government for killing hundreds of Witnesses, the Watchtower's unfeeling, actually grotesque policies for their own people caused many of their problems. The Watchtower seems to create situations to cause persecution because they feel that this benefits them in the long run.

For one who makes a living in science and medicine as myself, it is especially disconcerting to read articles in Watchtower publications advocating medical fraud or quackery (www.premier1.net/~raines/hate.html).

Not surprisingly, it appears the WS holds other secrets that only participants are aware of. Clearly, it is one thing to acknowledge that God is, rightfully, the final judge; but it is something else entirely to presume to be His instruments of justice, or to provide the "climate" for such "justice" by teaching hatred of those one considers, without warrant, to be His enemies. Jehovah's Witnesses are certainly not alone in this kind of egregious teaching, but such teachings do raise clear ethical concerns by themselves and in their implications.

The Jehovah's Witnesses and Mental Illness

It is often claimed by Jehovah's Witnesses that they are the "happiest and most content" people on earth, that their families are more successful than others, and that "they have the least need for psychiatrists."[406] Unfortunately, this is not true. Witnesses often have emotional problems. Disfellowshipped Witnesses (there are many) are regarded as "dead" by active members and even frequently by their own families. It goes without saying that this could produce severe emotional stress.[407] We reproduce, in part (with permission), "Jehovah's Witness and Mental Illness," an article written by Christian psychiatrist Dr. John Stedman (pen name), who has had an interest in the field of Jehovah's Witnesses' mental health for a number of years. He begins by noting the common knowledge of Jehovah's Witnesses mental health problems and the sect's denial of them:

> Psychiatrists and others who have worked with Jehovah's Witnesses have been aware for a number of years that both the mental illness rate and the suicide rate is very high among the Witnesses....Indeed the rate is so high that some hospitals are literally "stuffed with JW's"—one mental hospital is nicknamed "The Watchtower House" because the number of JW's is so high.
>
> This is common knowledge and the reasons are generally well known among mental health personnel,

but when the typical JW is confronted with this information he often violently refuses to acknowledge its validity.[408]

There is extreme Witness reluctance to submit their faith to the confines of a psychiatric setting. Since a Witness is by definition a happy, well-adjusted person, the Witness who has problems assumes that the fault is his, not the Society's. The true number of troubled Witnesses is unknown because those who seek help often shift the blame. "As discussed, the reporting probably represents much lower rates than actually is the case."[409] Stedman continues:

> Most Witnesses who are forced to seek psychiatric services are extremely reluctant to admit they are a Witness. A large number of JW's whom the writer has worked with put down "Protestant" or even "none" instead of their true affiliation. JW's are typically extremely ashamed of the fact that they are mentally ill and often will not be open and honest with the therapist because of the fear that his illness may bring reproach upon the Wt. Society.[410]

Subsequent research has confirmed the severity of the situation. As Dr. Jerry Bergman wrote in "Paradise Postponed...And Postponed: Why Jehovah's Witnesses Have a High Mental Illness":

> Several academic studies have explored the problem of mental illness among the Witnesses....Licensed therapist Havor Montague monitored the admissions to state and private mental hospitals and local mental health clinics in Ohio from 1972 to 1976. From this study of 102 cases, he estimated, "the mental illness rate of JWs is approximately 10 to 16 times higher than the rate for the general, non-Witness population....About 10% of the publishers (full members) in the average congregation are in serious need of professional help... [although they are often] able to hide this fact quite well, especially from outsiders."...Another study was completed in 1985 by

Robert Potter as part of a Ph.D. thesis on religion and mental health. He concluded that there exists "a strong positive correlation between Witness membership and clinical schizophrenia."...In addition, a 1985 German study by Elmer Koppl came to similar conclusions, as did a study by Norwegian psychologist Kjell Totland. Using Oakland County, Michigan, court records from 1965 to 1973, this writer found that not only is the mental illness rate above average, but the suicide and crime rates are also high, especially aggressive crimes against persons. (See also the *British Journal of Psychiatry,* June 1975; the *American Journal of Psychiatry,* March 1949; *Social Compass,* Vol. 24 [1977]; and Kjell Totland, "The Mental Health of Jehovah's Witnesses," *Journal of the Norwegian Psychological Association,* 1999.)

Bergman attributes the high mental illness rate to a variety of factors, including the extreme emphasis upon door-to-door witnessing, which can require, in addition to one's normal job, 20 to 30 hours per week. He also cites WS prohibitions against normal social relations and most school activities for children who, not infrequently, grow up lonely and troubled because the WS has not issued proper guidelines to help them live their lives. He concludes that the average Witness serves the Watchtower, not God, because serving the Watchtower is serving God. "Discouraged from many normal means of self-fulfillment, Witnesses slavishly devote their time and energy to serving an organization that does not care about them as individuals....Many feel they are trapped in a way of life in which virtually every alternative is undesirable." When WS service does not satisfy or solve one's problems, this, Bergman writes, causes guilt, leading "Witnesses to feel that they are evil and will not survive Armageddon. The depression and hopelessness have led to a disproportionate number of suicides and homicides among Witnesses."[411]

28

WHAT ARE SOME TIPS FOR TALKING WITH MEMBERS?

> If we want to worship God acceptably, we must know the truth. This is an important issue. Our eternal happiness depends on it. Therefore, everyone should ask himself: "Is my way of worship acceptable to God? Am I genuinely interested in learning the truth of God's Word? Or am I afraid of what a careful investigation might reveal?" (Watchtower Society website, "Do You Know the Truth?" April 1, 1999.)

Anyone talking with Jehovah's Witnesses will sooner than later discover they avoid examining works critical of the WS. This is because the leadership at Bethel headquarters has told members that they are to avoid critical materials as they would pornography (the *Watchtower,* March 15, 1986, p. 12). The reason is clear: their eternal life is at stake if they become deceived by the devil's teachings.

By insulating Witnesses from critical materials, the WS intends to ensure that members hear only what Society leaders wish them to hear. The quote beginning this section may be cited to members, in particular the last sentence. The WS cannot logically expect its membership to engage in "careful investigation" and simultaneously prohibit it by requiring members to investigate only WS materials. Clearly, only people who have something to fear demand intolerance toward responsible opposition literature. As a result, time spent thinking on how best to drive this point home may prove rewarding.

While the vast majority of active Witnesses probably will not read critical literature, some for different reasons will, and if so, this book or additional literature mentioned in the Authors' Note at the beginning of this book may be suggested.

Until recently, the Witnesses have largely avoided engaging in scholarly apologetic dialogue. The 1998 publication of Greg

Stafford's *Jehovah's Witnesses Defended: An Answer to Scholars and Critics* might signal a turning point. Despite the book's failing to make its case, it is probably the best Witness apologetic to date. Stafford does not make his case because he is still attempting to defend the indefensible: for example, biblical unitarianism and its denial of the Trinity. There are arguments here new to most Witnesses, and so reading his book may be useful for those engaged in regular contact and discussion. Dr. James White points out, in his review published in the *Christian Research Journal*, Vol. 21, No. 2 (1999, p. 49), that a basic flaw is Stafford's assumption that the terms "God," "Jehovah," and "Father" refer to the same person (unitarianism); thus if Jesus is not the person of the Father, He cannot be God. But to prove that the Son is not the Father only proves that the person of the Son is not the person of the Father, not that the Son is not deity. The doctrine of the Trinity holds that one divine essence—the one Being of God—is shared by the persons of the Father, the Son, and the Holy Spirit: three persons or centers of consciousness in one divine essence. Therefore, proving Jesus is not the Father is only proving biblical teaching. What Stafford needed to do was prove that Jesus is not deity, and in this he can only fail.

Interestingly, there appear to be some cracks in the new WS apologetic approach, at least with Stafford. According to *Apologia Report* (April 22, 2002), his new book, *Three Dissertations on the Teachings of Jehovah's Witnesses* (2002), while still attempting vainly to support WS teachings on the Trinity, nevertheless critiques and challenges other cherished WS doctrines, including blood transfusions, the spiritual authority of the Watchtower leaders, WS legalism, and others.

Our approach in this section will be to familiarize readers with a sampling of WS argumentation. Jehovah's Witnesses are one of the few groups trained in argumentation,[412] which is why we will cite specific illustrations.

The reason we have spent so much time documenting the Watchtower Society's fatal unreliability—its biased translation of the Bible, errors in prophecy, changing positions regarding divine revelation, contradictions in doctrines, interpretation, and so on—is because it is logically impossible to remain a Jehovah's Witness once faith in the Watchtower Society as "God's channel" has been undermined. Members can at least be encouraged to investigate this subject on their own using Watchtower magazine reprints, first editions of WS literature, and so on. Of course, if they will not read a critical text to at least find the alleged errors, they will have to read much more widely to find them on their own.

As noted, Witnesses have "answers" for WS problems, which appear to satisfy most members.[413] In the area of prophecy they may admit to a "few" errors, and the Witness who does not take the time to see how extensive these "few" errors are will remain loyal. "Progressive revelation" may explain doctrinal "refinements" if one never takes the time to see that the "refinements" are flat out denials of earlier doctrine. For "true believers," the solution to problems is not, unfortunately, the facts, but the will to believe. By whatever means, members may defend their beliefs with reasons that appear satisfying to them, but the issue remains the illegitimacy of WS authority and its counterarguments the in face of such damaging evidence. The fact that virtually all Greek scholars recognize the Society's *New World Translation* as biased, in error, and unscholarly is no less damning than its perfect failure in prophecy. The issue is not can they come up with ever new reasons for explaining their failures, but whether the level of failure is already sufficient to disprove WS claims to any impartial party.

Isaiah 9:6 is a case in point. It clearly refers to the Messiah (whom the WS acknowledges is Jesus Christ) as "Mighty God" (NWT). The Hebrew is *el gibbor*, "el" being a common name for Jehovah God. One might think this were enough. But for Jehovah's Witnesses, the Messiah simply cannot be God because of their theological presuppositions as to the unitarian nature of God. Therefore they reply, "It is true Jesus is *a* Mighty god, but not *Al*mighty God Jehovah. Only if Isaiah said Jesus were the

*Al*mighty God would it be saying Jesus is God." But if a descriptive prefix "Al" denotes a qualitative difference in nature between Jesus and Jehovah, then it must also be true that Jehovah must be inferior to Jesus on the same reasoning: Jehovah is merely "the Shepherd" in Psalm 23:1. But Jesus is the great Shepherd in Hebrews 13:20 and the Chief Shepherd in 1 Peter 5:4.

Obviously, the context must determine the use of words, and in Isaiah 9:6 the term "Mighty God" is asserting Jesus' deity. Both the original language and the context demand this conclusion. Rather than accept this, the Witnesses will find a reason for evading it: "At Isaiah 9:6 Jesus Christ is prophetically called 'El Gib.bohr, 'Mighty God' (not 'El Shad.day which applies to Jehovah at Genesis 17:1). 'El is used of idol gods at Psalm 81:9."[414] The reasoning is that since El Shaddai is used only of Jehovah and never of Jesus (which is true), Jesus cannot be God. But this does not logically follow. The fact that "El Shaddai" is not used of Jesus is irrelevant if Jesus is clearly declared God in Isaiah 9:6 and elsewhere. They also mention that the definite article is not used, but it is also missing in Isaiah 10:21, which is clearly a reference to Jehovah. Further, "el" may be used of the one true God or false gods, but in Isaiah 9:6 it can only refer to the true God: "...the Hebrew word 'el' in Isaiah usually denotes Jehovah, the only true God; when it does not do so (in 44:10,15,17; 45:20; 46:6), it is used to describe an idol made by men's hands. Surely Isaiah did not intend to say that the coming Messiah would be an idol god! It ought also be noted that the expression 'el gib-bohr' is in Old Testament literature a traditional designation of Jehovah—see Deuteronomy 10:17; Jeremiah 32:18; and Nehemiah 9:32."[415] The larger context is also relevant; for example, in Isaiah 10:21 Jehovah is described as "Mighty God," the exact phrase used to describe Jesus in Isaiah 9:6.

The Witnesses' response? They will drop the issue and find another argument. For example, they may point out this verse also calls Jesus "eternal Father." If orthodoxy does not believe Jesus is the person of the Father, then why believe He is literally the

Mighty God? The point missed is that Jesus is also a father to us if He is God, who is our Father (Psalm 103:13), and as such it is proper to describe Him as a father. (Nowhere does Isaiah or any scripture teach that the Person of the Son is the Person of the Father.) The same argument is true for the designation "eternal." Only if He is God is it proper to refer to Him as eternal. But is it proper to describe Him as "Mighty God" if He is not God? Clearly, it is not.

If the Watchtower Society itself has admitted that it makes errors and is not infallible, how much more important is it that a member think for himself and be willing to examine critically what he has been taught? To cite an illustration, one day at the brake shop we notice a man with the same model car we have. We also notice that the mechanic is putting in the wrong brake system, a mistake which could have fatal consequences. We tell this to the car owner, but he assures us the mechanic is qualified because he has read the owner's manual carefully. We tell him, "We have read it carefully ourselves, and this is the wrong brake system; your life and others will be in peril if you drive your car." Unless the owner will actually read the manual for himself and carefully study it to see who is correct, he could be making a fatal error. Claims and counterclaims can be made all day long. The individual must study these issues for himself. Even if the mechanic did have some apparent explanation for his interpreta-tion of the manual, once a red flag is raised, the manufacturer or other qualified mechanics need to be consulted.

Note some examples of what happens when a Jehovah's Witness studies the Bible on his own:

> After I looked through the publications and found other similar problems, I set them aside and began studying the Bible without literature aids of any kind. I read chapter by chapter, looking up cross references wherever necessary. The Holy Spirit revealed many things to me, and I was amazed to find that orthodox Christianity was really true. I discovered that the

Bible taught such doctrines as: the Trinity, the deity of Christ, the personality of the Holy Spirit, the immortality of the soul, and the visible return of Christ—*all* the doctrines the Watchtower Society had brainwashed us into rejecting![416]

Of course after doing a bit of background reading I began to see the utter temporal relativism of W.T. truth. Conflicting doctrines were held at various times, all with the infallible authority of Jehovah behind them....

I spent most of my life in an organization of HATE, until now I feel like a bird out of a cage. Keep a bird in a cage for twenty-five years, then turn it out, it is slow learning to fly again....I have been taught the Watchtower language so long I feel very weak in learning the language of love.[417]

One potentially useful approach may be to read the *New World Translation* and find areas that clearly teach biblical truths, which the Witness may then be challenged to believe. (Not every "error" has been corrected or addressed in WS literature.) Obviously, one will need a *New World Translation* to use these scriptures. (If their translation has changed from what we cite, seek the reason and ask them to justify the change. Were they wrong in the previous translation? Then what about the present translation?) Here are numerous passages from the NWT that can be used.

Salvation by faith alone. Titus 3:5; Ephesians 2:8-9; 2 Timothy 1:9; Romans 3:28, 4:5, 5:9, 6:23; John 6:29, 5:24; 1 John 3:14.

Christ as God (for example, Redeemer, Creator). John 1:3; John 5:18,23 with 19:7; Zechariah 11:13; John 1:2; Matthew 3:3; Micah 5:2 with Psalm 102:12 and Isaiah 40:28.

How many Lord of lords? Deuteronomy 10:17; Revelation 19:16. There is only one. Witnesses will say Jesus is Lord of lords on earth but not in heaven. Yet in Revelation 19:11,14, where is Jesus when John called Him Lord of lords but in heaven?

Who was with the Israelites? In Deuteronomy 32:12 it is Jehovah. In Deuteronomy 32:15 Jehovah is the Rock. In Isaiah 44:8, there is no other Rock. In 1 Corinthians 10:1-4, the Rock was Christ. Their interlinear shows that their translation is unjustified in translating "the rock-mass meant the Christ" (compare Romans 9:33). *Petra* means rock (rock-mass is an attempt to avoid the similarity to Deuteronomy 32:12). Their own Greek is translated as "was," not "meant." The Rock was Christ (that is, based on the previous Scriptures, Christ is deity).

Who is the Eternal Light? In Isaiah 60:19-20, it is Jehovah. In Revelation 21:23, it is Jesus (compare Revelation 22:5).

Who sits in the center of Jehovah's Throne? In Revelation 7:10-12, it is Jehovah. In Revelation 7:17, it is Jesus. *Meson* means center or middle of, the NWT "midst" is less clear but to the point.

Who sheds the light in the new Jerusalem? In Revelation 22:5, it is Jehovah. In Revelation 21:23, it is Jesus. (Other examples of Christ's deity can be found in the *New World Translation.* Any systematic theology or topical Bible can be used to check which verses in the *New World Translation* teach this.)

Eternal punishment. Daniel 12:2 and Revelation 20:10. That Revelation 20:10 is not symbolic, as maintained by the NWT, is seen by the Greek word translated "tormented." It is the same word in Matthew 8:6,19 and Revelation 14:11, which means literal torment. The Greek word "for ever and ever" is the same word used in Hebrews 1:8, which the Witnesses interpret as referring to Jehovah and must therefore mean eternal. Also, see the *Kingdom Interlinear* at Jude 7. And in Hebrews 10:28-29, the one who tramples underfoot the blood of Jesus receives a *worse* judgment than death. How can there be a "much more severe punishment" than death, which is only annihilation to Witnesses? To receive a worse punishment than death, the spirit must remain alive.

The deity of the Holy Spirit. Acts 5:3-4; Hebrews 10:15; Hebrews 3:7; Isaiah 6:8-9 with Acts 28:25-26; Isaiah 40:28 with 1 Corinthians 2:10-11; Isaiah 63:10 with Psalm 78:17.

Assurance of salvation. 1 John 5:13; John 6:39,47; Romans 8:1.

Everyone needs spiritual rebirth. 1 John 5:1 and related passages.

The personality of the Holy Spirit. John 14:26; 16:13; Acts 16:6-7; 10:19; 1 Corinthians 2:10; 12:11; John 14:16,26; 15:26; 16:7; Romans 8:26-27; Acts 13:4; Matthew 28:19; Ephesians 4:30; Matthew 12:31; Acts 5:3; 7:51; Hebrews 10:29.

Immediate judgment at death (no second chance). John 5:28-29; 13:18.

A related approach, in this case with the doctrine of the Trinity, was given in our *The Facts on Jehovah's Witnesses,* (pp. 12–13), which we will reproduce. "The doctrine of the Trinity can be seen from five simple statements supported by the Bible." (The following scriptures taken from the Jehovah's Witnesses' *New World Translation,* 1970 ed., are abbreviated "NWT.")[418]

There is only one true God. "For there is one God, and one mediator between God and men...." (1 Timothy 2:5 NWT; compare Deuteronomy 4:35; 6:4; Isaiah 43:10).

The Father is God. "There is actually to us one God the Father...." (1 Corinthians 8:6 NWT; compare John 17:1-3; 2 Corinthians 1:3; Philippians 2:11; Colossians 1:3; 1 Peter 1:2).

Jesus Christ, the Son, is God. "But he [Jesus] was also calling God his own Father, making himself equal to God" (John 5:18 NWT). "In answer Thomas said to him [Jesus]: 'My Lord and my God!'" (John 20:28 NWT; compare Isaiah 9:6; John 1:1; Romans 9:5; Titus 2:13; 2 Peter 1:1; see note 418).

The Holy Spirit is a Person, is eternal, and is therefore God. The Holy Spirit is a Person: "However, when that one arrives, the spirit of the truth, *he* will guide you into all the truth, for *he* will not speak of *his* own impulse, but what things *he* hears *he* will speak, and *he* will declare to you the things coming" (John 14:13 NWT, emphasis added). The Holy Spirit is *eternal:* "How much more will the blood of the Christ, who through an everlasting spirit offered himself without blemish to God...(Hebrews 9:14 NWT). The Holy Spirit is *therefore God:* "But Peter said: 'Ananias, why has Satan emboldened you to play false to the holy spirit....You have played false, not to men, but to God' " (Acts 5:3-4 NWT).

The Father, Son, and Holy Spirit are distinct Persons. "Baptizing them in the name of the Father and of the Son and of the holy spirit"; "the undeserved kindness of the Lord Jesus Christ and the love of God and the sharing in the holy spirit be with all of you" (Matthew 28:19; 2 Corinthians 13:14 NWT).

It is clear from these verses, read either from the NWT or a modern version like the New International Version, that the Bible teaches the one true God exists eternally as Father, Son, and Holy Spirit.

Yet another approach is to discuss individual scriptures with open members, knowing their response beforehand and having thought through a reply. Samples are provided here.

John 20:28 (NWT). Thomas' response to Jesus as "My God" is not clear enough for Witnesses. The standard response is that Thomas did not mean "my only *true* God," or else Jesus would have reproved him. Thomas really meant that Jesus was the Son of God, or that he was only using this as a figure of speech intended as respect towards Christ. But in John 5:18 and John 10:30, the apostle John makes no qualifying note stating Jesus attempted to correct other people's "misperception" of Him as God. This would be a serious error in an inerrant Bible. Also, Thomas did not say "My Son of God," but rather "My God." The Greek is *ho theos mou,* "the God of me"; that is, my God. What else can "My God" mean but "my only true God"? Thomas was not a polytheist. Jesus recognized only one true God, and He did not rebuke Thomas for calling Him God.

John 10:30-33. Jehovah's Witnesses will say that by "I and the Father are one" Jesus meant, "I and the Father are one in purpose and unity," even though this is not what the verse says. The neuter (*hen*) teaches one in essence. Clearly the Jews understood the claim, for they would not seek to stone Him (a capital offense) for merely claiming to be one in purpose with God. They would, however, stone Jesus for alleged blaspheming, for falsely claiming to be God. The NWT mistranslates John 10:33 as "a god." As their interlinear indicates, *poieis seauton theos* is without the article, hence underneath the Greek text, the English reads "making yourself God." (The distinction between capital and non-capital letters was not made in the Greek.)

Jesus did not try to convince the Jews that they had misunderstood Him here. He simply reasserted His deity. In John 10:34-38, He reasoned that if even Scripture calls men "gods" figuratively, how can the very One whom the Father sanctified and sent into the world (by virgin birth, that is, as the prophesied divine Messiah) be blaspheming when He claims to be God's only Son and does the miracles that prove His claims? Even the NWT claims at John 19:7 that to be God's Son meant claiming to be God. In other words, Jesus is saying, "If it is possible for anyone to claim equality with God, it is possible for Me. I came from the Father, I do His works, and We are one." Jesus then says, "If I am not doing the works of my Father (doing God's works, doing the works only God can do) do not believe Me"; that is, do not believe that "I and the Father are one" in essence. "But if I am doing the works, at least believe them, that you may know that I and the Father are one" (that is, that He is God).

John 14:28. Jesus said that the Father was greater than He was. This verse teaches the Father was greater than Jesus in His human incarnation and servant role. Jesus had by His own volition humbled and limited Himself (Philippians 2:6-7). The Father was greater in that Jesus submitted to Him, but mere submission does not demand inferiority as to nature, whether in the Godhead or among men and women in Christian marriage or between a king and his subjects. The Greek *meizon* implies a quantitative aspect. If John meant "inferior" he should have used *kreitton*, which means qualitatively better, as is used in Hebrews 1:4.

Revelation 3:14. Dr. Bruce Metzger comments,

> The New World Translation...is also in error at Revelation 3:14, where it makes the exalted Christ refer to himself as "the beginning of the creation by God." The Greek text of this verse...is far from saying that Christ was created by God, for the genitive case... means "of God" and not "by God," which would require the preposition....Actually the word *arche*, translated "beginning," carries with it the Pauline idea expressed in Colossians 1:15-18, and signifies that Christ is the origin, or primary source, of God's creation (compare also John 1:3, "Apart from him not even one thing came into existence").[419]

Hebrews 1:8-10. We have noted that Hebrews 1:8 in the NWT is a biased translation. We have not noted that Hebrews 1:10 refers to Jesus, as clearly evidenced by the conjunction "and" (NWT). But Hebrews 1:10 is a quote of Psalm 102:25, referring to Jehovah creating the world. Here this Scripture is applied to Jesus. We might also observe the Greek word *charakter* in Hebrews 1:3 ("exact representation of his very being" NWT). The Greek word was taken from a word used to describe an impression produced by a seal or a die stamp in wax or metal. Moulton and Milligan defined it as "an exact reproduction."[420] If Jesus is the "exact reproduction" of Jehovah, is He merely a creature? The answer is that He and His Father are indeed One.

Nehemiah 9:6. Here all the angels of heaven worship Jehovah alone. In Luke 4:8 worship is to be given to God only. In

Hebrews 1:6 Jesus receives angelic worship. How can Jesus receive the worship of the angels if He is only a created angel Himself?

John 17:22. Jesus received glory from God. The Witnesses reply, "Can God receive glory from God"? But there are different types of glory. For example, Jesus' essential glory is the glory of His deity, which cannot be communicated. His moral glory is the glory of His character, and His acquired glory is the glory received through His incarnation, death, and resurrection. Clearly, the glory Jesus received from God was the glory of His incarnation and His death, the commission to save believers (John 5:36,44; 17:4-5), not the glory of His innate deity, which He could never receive and which He had with the Father before the world was (John 17:5).

John 20:17. Jesus said, "I ascend to My God." The Witnesses reply, "If he were God how could he refer to 'His God'?" As a true man, Jesus could properly speak of God as "My God," just as through the virgin birth He could speak of God as "My Father."

Other verses could be listed, but these are sufficient to illustrate that the Watchtower Society's scriptural apologetic is insufficient to warrant trust.

Finally, in any discussion with the Witnesses, it should be remembered that they have little or no assurance of salvation. Someone who has this assurance and can communicate it biblically will present an attractive alternative. M.J. Schnell remarks: "Assurance of salvation is prized amidst Jehovah's Witnesses. You work hard for it. But as you perform one task, other tasks loom ahead and you are never sure. For thirty years I sought assurance in this manner. I had not found it."[421] Members of Jehovah's Witnesses thus need to know the blessed truth that: "I write these things to you who believe in the name of the Son of God so that you may *know* that you have eternal life" (1 John 5:13, emphasis added; compare John 6:47).

Even the Watchtower Society agrees that "sincere seekers for the truth want to know what is right. They realize that they would only be fooling themselves if they rejected portions of God's Word while claiming to base their beliefs on other parts."[422]

29

A PERSONAL WORD TO JEHOVAH'S WITNESSES

What can you do if you desire to live for God and Christ and yet are unsure about what you have been taught?

First, don't be discouraged. Don't give up on God because someone lied to you. Perhaps you accepted the Watchtower's claims without first testing them carefully. Possibly your own doubts and discouragement will become the means by which God leads you into the truth and into a personal relationship with Him. And in addition, as a way to help others.

Second, realize that you aren't alone. Millions of others were disfellowshipped or left the Watchtower organization.[423] It's not the end of the world. (Thankfully!)

Third, take the initiative and obtain the truth for yourself. The Watchtower has told you before that "sincere seekers for the truth want to know what is right."[424] If you study the Bible on your own, in humility before God, God says that He Himself will show you the truth:

> But if any of you lacks wisdom, let him ask of God, who gives to all men generously and without reproach, and it will be given to him....Draw near to God and He will draw near to you (James 1:5; 4:8 NASB).

Ask Him, and He will help you. Believe and obey His Word without altering it, and you will know the truth and, as Jesus promised, "the truth will make you free" (John 8:31-32).

Fourth, accept God's loving and free gift of salvation in Christ Jesus. There are no works to earn it! It is entirely a gift. God never intended for you to spend your life in a hopeless, never-ending attempt to earn your own salvation by measuring up to His standard of perfection. He has already told us that it is impossible for any person to do so. Because of your fallen nature, you can't do it (Romans 8:3). "But because of His great love for us, God, who is rich in mercy, made us alive with Christ even when we were dead in transgressions—it is by grace you have been saved" (Ephesians 2:4-5). The really good news that God gives to all of us is:

> Therefore, there is now no condemnation for those who are in Christ Jesus (Romans 8:1).

> You see, at just the right time, when we were still powerless, Christ died for the ungodly (Romans 5:6).

> But the gift of God is eternal life in Christ Jesus our Lord (Romans 6:23).

> However, to the man who does not work [for salvation] but trusts God who justifies the wicked, his faith is credited as righteousness (Romans 4:5).

> So we, too, have put our faith in Christ Jesus that we may be justified by faith in Christ and not by observing the law, because by observing the law no one will be justified....I do not set aside the grace of God, for if righteousness could be gained through the law, Christ died for nothing! (Galatians 2:16,21).

Fifth, God wants you to confess your sins and accept the forgiveness He provided through Christ's shed blood. Read Isaiah 55:1-3 and see how eagerly God longs for you to come to Him to rest. Do you long for eternal life and the assurance of it? God's Word says you can know that you have it:

> The one who believes in the Son of God has the witness in himself; the one who does not believe God has made Him a liar, because he has not believed in the witness that God has borne concerning His Son. And the witness is this, that God has *given* us eternal life, and this life is in His Son. *He who has the Son has the*

life; he who does not have the Son of God *does not* have the life. These things I have written to you who believe in the name of the Son of God, in order that *you may know that you have eternal life* (1 John 5:10-13 NASB, emphasis added).

You can receive the gift of salvation right now by praying sincerely something like the following:

Dear God, right now, I'm confused. But I earnestly long to know You and serve You as You really are. Please reveal Yourself to me. I confess that I'm a sinner and incapable of earning merit in Your eyes. I believe Jesus' words, "You must be born again." I now receive Jesus Christ as my personal Lord and Savior. I receive Him as my God. I commit myself to Him and to Your Word. Please help me to understand Your Word correctly. Amen.

WATCHTOWER DOCTRINAL SUMMARY

God: Unipersonal; His proper name is Jehovah.

Jesus: A created angel who has existed in three stages or phases (the archangel Michael, Jesus of Nazareth, an exalted archangel Michael).

The Christ: The anointed one; Jesus became "the Christ" at His baptism, at which point He was also spiritually reborn.

Holy Spirit: The impersonal active force of Jehovah.

Trinity: A pagan superstition devised by Satan to blaspheme Jehovah and lead people astray.

Salvation: By faith and works. (Man is capable of achieving salvation without spiritual re-birth.)

Man: A material (not spiritual) creation of Jehovah.

Satan: Generally orthodox teaching, except for the fact of Satan's annihilation and Watchtower Society confusion over good and evil angels.

Second Coming: Occurred invisibly in 1874 (later changed to 1914).

Bible: Authoritative only when interpreted by the Watchtower Society.

Death: Death brings annihilation—temporary for those "resurrected" (re-created) to life, eternal for the wicked.

Heaven and hell: Heaven is a place reserved for only the 144,000 "elect"; the idea of an eternal hell is a "doctrine of demons."

APPENDIX
LETTER OF DR. JULIUS R. MANTEY TO THE WATCHTOWER SOCIETY

"I haven't read any translation that is as diabolical and as damnable as the JW so-called translation.... They (the Society) hate Jesus Christ."

—Dr. Julius Mantey; "Distortions of the New Testament," Tape "T-2," available from Witness, Inc., Clayton, CA

July 11, 1974
Watchtower Bible & Tract Society
117 Adams St.
Brooklyn, New York 11201

Dear Sirs:

I have a copy of your letter addressed to *Caris* in Santa Ana, California, and I am writing to express my disagreement with statements made in that letter, as well as in quotations you have made from the Dana-Mantey Greek Grammar.

(1) Your statement: "their work allows for the rendering found in the *Kingdom Interlinear Translation of the Greek Scriptures* at John 1:1." There is no statement in our grammar that was ever meant to imply that "a god" was a permissible translation in John 1:1.

A. We had no "rule" to argue in support of the trinity.

B. Neither did we state that we did have such intention. We were simply delineating the facts inherent in Biblical language.

C. Your quotation from p. 148 (3) was in a paragraph under the heading: "*With the Subject in a Copulative sentence.*" Two examples occur there to illustrate that "the article points out the subject in these examples." But we made no statement in this paragraph about the predicate except that, "as it stands the other persons of the trinity may be implied in *theos.*" And isn't that the opposite of what your translation "a god" infers? You quoted me out of context. On pages 139 and 149 (VI) in our grammar we stated: "without the article *theos* signifies divine essence...*theos en ho logos* emphasizes Christ's participation in the essence of the divine nature." Our interpretation is in agreement with that in NEB and the TEV: "What God was, the Word was"; and with that of Barclay: "The nature of the Word was the same as the nature of God," which you quoted in your letter to *Caris.*

(2) Since Colwell's and Harner's articles in *JBL* [*Journal of Biblical Literature*], especially that of Harner, it is neither scholarly nor reasonable to translate John 1:1 "The Word was a god." Word-order has made obsolete and incorrect such a rendering.

(3) Your quotation of Colwell's Rule is inadequate because it quotes only a part of his findings. You did not quote this strong assertion: "A predicate nominative which precedes the verb cannot be translated as an indefinite or a 'qualitative' noun solely because of the absence of the article."

(4) Prof. Harner, vol. 92:1 (1973) in *JBL*, has gone beyond Colwell's research and has discovered that anarthrous predicate nouns preceding the verb function primarily to express the nature or character of the subject. He found this true in 53 passages in the Gospel of John and 8 in the Gospel of Mark. Both scholars wrote that when indefiniteness was intended the gospel writers

regularly placed the predicate noun after the verb, and both Colwell and Harner have stated that *theos* in John 1:1 is not indefinite and should not be translated "a god." Watchtower writers appear to be the only ones advocating such a translation now. The evidence appears to be 99% against them.

(5) Your statement in your letter that the sacred text itself should guide one and "not just someone's rule book." We agree with you. But our study proves that Jehovah's Witnesses do the opposite of that whenever the "sacred text" differs with their heretical beliefs. For example the translation of *kolasis* as "*cutting off*" when punishment is the only meaning cited in the lexicons for it. The mistranslation of *ego eimi* as "I have been" in John 8:58. The addition of "for all time" in Hebrews 9:27 when nothing in the Greek New Testament supports it. The attempt to belittle Christ by mistranslating *arche tes ktiseos* "beginning of the creation" when he is magnified as "the creator of all things" (John 1:2) and as "equal with God" (Philippians 2:6) before he humbled himself and lived in a human body here on earth. Your quotation of "The Father is greater than I am" (John 14:28) to prove that Jesus was not equal to God overlooks the fact stated in Philippians 2:6-8, when Jesus said that he was still in his voluntary state of humiliation. That state ended when he ascended to heaven. Why the attempt to deliberately deceive people by mispunctuation by placing a comma after "today" in Luke 23:43 when in the Greek, Latin, German and all English translations except yours, *even in the Greek in your KIT,* the comma occurs after *lego* (I say)——— "Today you will be with me in Paradise." 2 Corinthians 5:8, "to be out of the body and at home with the Lord." These passages teach that the redeemed go immediately to heaven [after] death, which does not agree with your teachings that death ends all life until the resurrection. Cf. Psalm 23:6 and Hebrews 1:10.

The above are only a few examples of Watchtower mistranslations and perversions of God's Word.

In view of the preceding facts, especially because you have been quoting me out of context, I herewith request you not to quote the *Manual Grammar of the Greek New Testament* again, which you have been doing for 24 years. Also that you not quote it or me in any of your publications from this time on.

Also that you publicly and immediately apologize in the Watchtower magazine, since my words had no relevance to the absence of the article before *theos* in John 1:1. And please write to *Caris* and state that you misused and misquoted my "rule."

On the page before the *Preface* in the grammar are these words: "All rights reserved—no part of this book may be reproduced in any form without permission in writing from the publisher."

If you have such permission, please send me a photocopy of it.

If you do not heed these requests you will suffer the consequences.

Regretfully yours,
Julius R. Mantey

NOTES

Note: All Jehovah's Witnesses texts are published by the Watchtower Bible and Tract Society (WBTS, 25 Columbia Heights, Brooklyn, NY 11021).

1. Walter Martin and Norman Klann, *Jehovah of the Watchtower* (Chicago: Moody Press, 1974), p. 15.
2. Based on *Yearbook* reports.
3. "2001 Report of Jehovah's Witnesses Worldwide"; cf. "1997 Report of Jehovah's Witnesses Worldwide" (1998).
4. See the 1999–2001 *Yearbooks*, the WS website (www.watchtower.org), and the "2001 Report of Jehovah's Witnesses Worldwide."
5. W.M. Nelson, R.K. Smith, "Jehovah's Witnesses Part II: Their Mission" in Hesselgrave (ed.), *Dynamic Religious Movements* (Grand Rapids, MI: Baker Book House, 1978), p. 192.
6. Edmond C. Gruss, *We Left Jehovah's Witnesses: A Non-Prophet Organization* (Nutley, NJ: Presbyterian & Reformed, 1992), p. 6.
7. Ibid., pp. 6-11.
8. Ibid., p. 11.
9. Raymond Franz, *Crisis of Conscience* (Atlanta: Commentary Press, 1983), p. 31.
10. J.K. Van Baalen, *Chaos of the Cults* (Grand Rapids, MI: Eerdmans), p. 257.
11. J.H. Gerstner, *The Theology of the Major Sects* (Grand Rapids, MI: Baker Book House, 1960), p. 29.
12. See "The Christadelphians" in the *Ankerberg Theological Research Institute News Magazine*, March/April 1999.
13. Edmund Gruss, *Apostles of Denial: An Examination and Exposé of the History, Doctrines and Claims of the Jehovah's Witnesses* (Grand Rapids, MI: Baker Book House, 1976), pp. 15-16.
14. Ibid., p. 14.
15. The *Watchtower*, July 15, 1906, p. 229; September 15, 1910, p. 298 (see B.J. Kotwall and B. Stett , "Flashes of Light," www.watchtowerinformationservice.org/flashes.html).
16. Gruss, *Apostles of Denial*, ch. 5.
17. Ibid., p. 76.
18. Ibid., pp. 19-33.
19. Ibid., p. 37.
20. Ibid., chs. 2-7.
21. Watchtower Bible & Tract Society, *God's Kingdom of a Thousand Years Has Approached* (Brooklyn: WBTS, 1973), p. 342.
22. *Watchtower*, July 15, 1960, p. 439, cited in Michael Van Buskirk, *The Scholastic Dishonesty of the Watchtower* (Santa Ana, CA: CARIS, 1976), p. 26.
23. *Watchtower*, May 15, 1980, pp. 17-18.
24. *Watchtower*, March 1, 1979, p. 16.
25. *Watchtower*, September 1, 1979, p. 21.
26. H. Montague, "Watchtower Congregations: Communion or Conflict," p. 7, published by CARIS, Costa Mesa, CA.

27. C.J. Woodsworth, G.H. Fisher (comp. and ed.), *The Finished Mystery* (Brooklyn: International Bible Students Assoc., 1918), p. 387.

28. Gerstner, *Theology*, p. 34, citing Stroup, *The Jehovah's Witnesses* (1945) citing Rutherford, *Why Serve Jehovah*, p. 62.

29. Gerstner, p. 34, citing Stroup, p. 125.

30. Anthony Hoekema, *The Four Major Cults* (Eerdmans, 1970), p. 245, emphasis Russell's.

31. Gruss, *We Left Jehovah's Witnesses*, p. 41.

32. Charles S. Braden, *These Also Believe: A Study of Modern American Cults and Minority Religious Movements*, (NY: MacMillan, 1970), p. 65.

33. Gerstner, *Theology*, pp. 34-35.

34. William Cetnar, "Why I Was Kicked Out of the Watchtower," *Eternity*, October 1980, p. 41.

35. *Watchtower*, November 1, 1961, p. 668.

36. *Watchtower*, October 1, 1967, p. 591.

37. *Watchtower*, February 1, 1952, p. 80. The previous three references are cited by Van Buskirk in *The Scholastic Dishonesty of the Watchtower*, pp. 24-26 in fuller quotations.

38. Russell, *Studies in the Scriptures*, Vol. 1 (1907), pp. 10-11, cited in Gruss, *Apostles of Denial*, p. 220.

39. Russell, *Studies in the Scriptures*, Vol. 1, p. 41, cited in Gruss, *Apostles of Denial*, p. 221.

40. Gruss, *Apostles of Denial*, p. 221.

41. *"The Word"—Who Is He According to John?* (1962), p. 7.

42. Watchtower Bible & Tract Society, *The Truth that Leads to Eternal Life* (Brooklyn: WTBS, 1968), pp. 22, 42; 1975 Yearbook, p. 36.

43. Gruss, *We Left Jehovah's Witnesses*, pp. 77-78.

44. Nelson and Smith, "Jehovah's Witnesses Part II," in Hesselgrave (ed.), *Dynamic Religious Movements: Case Studies of Rapidly Growing Religious Movements Around the World* (Grand Rapids, MI: Baker, 1978), p. 193.

45. Ibid.

46. Ibid., pp. 194-97.

47. H. Montague, "Watchtower Congregations: Communion or Conflict?" pp. 1-7, CARIS tract.

48. Ibid.

49. Ibid.

50. Ibid.

51. WS website, "How Can You Find the True Religion?" Lesson 13 (<www.watchtower.org>).

52. Montague, "Watchtower Congregations," pp. 1-7, CARIS tract.

53. For further reading, see our book *Fast Facts on Defending Your Faith* (Eugene, OR: Harvest House, 2002).

54. Gruss, *We Left Jehovah's Witnesses*, pp. 19, 22.

55. Gruss, *Apostles of Denial*, pp. 4-5; *The Watchtower*, April 15, 1978, p. 15.

56. For example, see *Paradise Restored*, p. 307; *The Nations Shall Know That I Am Jehovah—How?* pp. 6, 10.

57. Braden, *These Also Believe*, p. 380.

58. Hoekema, *Four Major Cults*, p. 285.

59. Martin, *Jehovah of the Watchtower*, p. 114.

60. J.F. Rutherford, commentator, *Preparation* (Brooklyn: Watch Tower Bible and Tract Society, 1933), pp. 19-20.

61. J.F. Rutherford, *Religion* (WBTS, 1940), p. 104, cited in Gruss, *Apostles of Denial*, p. 63.

62. J.F. Rutherford, *Enemies*, p. 118, cited in Gruss, *Apostles of Denial*, p. 63.

63. Ibid., p. 306, cited in Gruss, *Apostles of Denial*, p. 64.

64. *Watchtower*, September 1, 1979, p. 28.

65. *Watchtower*, November 1, 1976, p. 665.

66. *Watchtower*, July 1, 1980, p. 12.

67. Watchtower Bible & Tract Society, *Man's Salvation Out of World Distress at Hand!* (Brooklyn: WTBS, 1975), pp. 335, 216.

68. *Watchtower*, March 1, 1979, p. 18.

69. *Man's Salvation,* pp. 338-339, 226-227; *Watchtower,* March 1, 1980, p. 21.

70. *Man's Salvation,* p. 215.

71. *Watchtower,* September 1, 1979, p. 21.

72. *Watchtower,* November 1, 1979, p. 26; *Watchtower,* May 15, 1980, p. 27; *Watchtower,* August 15, 1979, p. 27.

73. *Watchtower,* September 1, 1979, p. 22.

74. Ibid., pp. 20-21.

75. *Watchtower,* December 1951, pp. 731-32, cited in Martin, *Jehovah of the Watchtower,* p. 106; *Watchtower,* September 1, 1979, p. 29.

76. Letter of August 1987.

77. *Watchtower,* September 15, 1910, p. 298, cited in *Reprints of the Original Watchtower and Herald of Christ's Presence,* p. 4685.

78. Gruss, *We Left Jehovah's Witnesses,* p. 7.

79. For example, cf. Rutherford, *Preparation,* pp. 343-44.

80. Hoekema, *Four Major Cults,* pp. 249-55.

81. *God's Kingdom,* p. 352.

82. Rutherford, *Preparation,* pp. 342-44.

83. Hoekema, *Four Major Cults,* p. 255.

84. Gruss, *Apostles of Denial,* ch. 11.

85. Ibid., pp. 238-39.

86. Watchtower Bible & Tract Society, *Make Sure of All Things; Hold Fast to What Is Fine* (Brooklyn: WTBS, 1965), p. 267.

87. Watchtower Bible & Tract Society, *Aid to Bible Understanding* (Brooklyn, NY: WBTS, 1971), p. 665.

88. *Make Sure,* p. 267.

89. W.M. Nelson, R.K. Smith, "Jehovah's Witnesses, Part II, Their Mission," in David Hesselgrave, *Dynamic Religious Movements,* p. 188.

90. Quoted in Nelson and Smith, ibid., in Hesselgrave, p. 181; *Studies in the Scriptures,* Vol. 7 (*The Finished Mystery*), p. 410.

91. *The Truth that Leads to Eternal Life,* p. 22; Watchtower Bible & Tract Society, *Then Is Finished the Mystery of God* (Brooklyn: WBTS, 1969), p. 10.

92. Watchtower Bible & Tract Society, *Things in Which It Is Impossible for God to Lie* (Brooklyn: WBTS, 1965), p. 256.

93. Rutherford, *Uncovered* (1937), pp. 48-49 cited in Braden, *These Also Believe,* p. 371.

94. *Let God Be True,* 2nd ed., p. 111, cited in Van Baalen, *The Chaos of the Cults,* p. 268.

95. *Things in Which It Is Impossible for God to Lie,* p. 259.

96. *"The Word"—Who Is He According to John?* p. 12.

97. *Let God be True* (1946, rev. 1952), p. 102, cited in Gruss, *Apostles of Denial,* p. 110.

98. Personal conversations with Jehovah's Witnesses. Incomprehensibility is not the same as irrationality.

99. Gruss, *Apostles of Denial,* pp. 101, 109-10.

100. *Aid to Bible Understanding,* p. 1152.

101. Ibid., p. 918.

102. Ibid., p. 920.

103. Ibid.

104. *The Truth Shall Make You Free* (1943), p. 246, cited in James Bjornstad, *Counterfeits at Your Door* (Glendale, CA: Regal, 1979), p. 67.

105. *Things in Which It Is Impossible for God to Lie,* p. 231.

106. Bjornstad, *Counterfeits at Your Door,* p. 68.

107. Hoekema, *Four Major Cults,* p. 272.

108. *Let God Be True* (1946, Rev. 1952), p. 74, cited in Hoekema, *Four Major Cults,* p. 295.

109. *Aid to Bible Understanding,* p. 437.

110. *Things in Which It Is Impossible for God to Lie,* p. 211.

111. Russell, *Studies in the Scriptures,* Vol. 5 (1906), p. 454.

112. *The Truth Shall Make You Free* (1943), p. 264, cited in Bjornstad, *Counterfeits*, p. 93.

113. Nelson and Smith, "Jehovah's Witnesses," in Hesselgrave, *Dynamic*, pp. 178-79.

114. Bjornstad, *Counterfeits at Your Door*, p. 67.

115. Ibid., p. 68; see also *Let Your Name be Sanctified* (1961), p. 272.

116. *Man's Salvation Out of World Distress*, pp. 42-43.

117. *Watchtower*, January 15, 1980, p. 31, emphasis added.

118. Bjornstad, *Counterfeits at Your Door*, pp. 92-94; see also *Make Sure of All Things*, p. 255.

119. Ibid.

120. *God's Kingdom of a Thousand Years*, p. 354; cf. *Man's Salvation Out of World Distress*, p. 42.

121. *Holy Spirit, The Force Behind the Coming New Order* (Brooklyn: WTBS, 1976), p. 11.

122. *Aid to Bible Understanding*, pp. 1543-44; *Watchtower*, November 1, 1976, p. 656.

123. *Aid to Bible Understanding*, pp. 1542-43.

124. *Things in Which It Is Impossible for God to Lie*, p. 269; "The Holy Spirit—God's Active Force," <www.watchtower.org/library/ti/article_07.htm>).

125. *Watchtower*, February 15, 1983, p. 12.

126. Anthony A. Hoekema, *Four Major Cults*, p. 269.

127. *Man's Salvation Out of World Distress at Hand!* (1975), p. 112.

128. Watchtower Bible and Tract Society, *Making Your Family Life Happy* (1978), pp. 182-83.

129. *Make Sure of All Things; Hold Fast to What Is Fine* (1965), p. 296.

130. Ibid., p. 297.

131. Ibid., p. 439.

132. Ibid.

133. *Aid to Bible Understanding* (1971), p. 1240.

134. *The Watchtower*, May 1, 1979, p. 15.

135. Ibid., p. 20.

136. *Watchtower*, June 15, 1977, p. 373.

137. *Watchtower*, May 1, 1980, p. 13.

138. Hoekema, *Four Major Cults*, pp. 282-83.

139. Ibid.

140. Ibid., pp. 284-85.

141. Ibid., p. 285.

142. Ibid.

143. Ibid.

144. *Christianity Today*, December 12, 1980, pp. 68-71.

145. *Aid to Bible Understanding* (1971), p. 437.

146. Watchtower Bible and Tract Society, *Life Everlasting in Freedom of the Sons of God* (1969), pp. 397-99.

147. Ibid., pp. 391-93, cf. pp. 396, 397.

148. Ibid., pp. 397-99.

149. Watchtower Bible and Tract Society, *You May Survive Armageddon into God's New World* (1955), pp. 357-60.

150. See Jerry Bergman, "Paradise Postponed...And Postponed: Why Jehovah's Witnesses Have a High Mental Illness Level," *Christian Research Journal*, Summer 1996.

151. Gruss, *We Left Jehovah's Witnesses*, p. 132.

152. Ibid.

153. *You May Survive Armageddon*, pp. 354-55.

154. *Aid to Bible Understanding*, p. 735.

155. *You May Survive Armageddon*, p. 355.

156. Ibid., p. 356.

157. Ibid., pp. 356-57.

158. Watchtower Bible and Tract Society, *From Paradise Lost to Paradise Regained* (1958), p. 238.

159. *Life Everlasting*, p. 400.

160. *Things in Which It Is Impossible for God to Lie* (1965), p. 396.

161. *Aid to Bible Understanding,* p. 1671.

162. *Things in Which It Is Impossible for God to Lie,* p. 401; pp. 401-04; *From Paradise Lost to Paradise Regained,* p. 152; see also pp. 242, 244, 246-47, 249.

163. Walter Martin and Norman Klann, *Jehovah of the Watchtower* (Chicago: Moody Press, 1974), p. 71.

164. Gruss, *Apostles of Denial,* p. 90.

165. Hoekema, *Four Major Cults,* pp. 276-79.

166. Gruss, *Apostles of Denial,* pp. 142-43.

167. *Aid to Bible Understanding,* p. 33; cf. *Let God Be True* (1946), p. 119, cited in Hoekema, *Four Major Cults,* p. 277.

168. *Aid to Bible Understanding,* p. 1373.

169. *From Paradise Lost,* p. 236.

170. *Things in Which It Is Impossible for God to Lie,* p. 232.

171. *You May Survive,* pp. 38-39.

172. *Aid to Bible Understanding,* p. 1373.

173. Hoekema, *Four Major Cults,* pp. 278-79.

174. Gruss, *Apostles of Denial,* p. 144.

175. Ibid., p. 145.

176. Gruss, *We Left Jehovah's Witnesses,* pp. 37-38.

177. Bjornstad, *Counterfeits,* p. 85, cites *New Heavens and a New Earth* (1953), pp. 147-48; *What Has Religion Done for Mankind?* (1951), pp. 240-45.

178. Bjornstad, *Counterfeits,* p. 85.

179. *You May Survive,* p. 357.

180. Martin, *Jehovah of the Watchtower,* pp. 71-72.

181. *Let God Be True* (1946, rev. 1952), p. 74.

182. *Aid to Bible Understanding,* pp. 1532-34.

183. Ibid., p. 1535.

184. Watchtower Bible and Tract Society, *Is This Life All There Is?* pp. 96-97, 119.

185. Ibid., pp. 115-16, 120.

186. *Make Sure of All Things,* pp. 226-27.

187. See John Weldon and Zola Levitt, *Psychic Healing* (Chicago: Moody Press, 1982), chapter on psychometry and radionics.

188. *Demonism and the Watchtower* (1969), p. 14. (Gruss believes that much of what Goodrich claims in this area is accurate—see Gruss, *Apostles of Denial,* p. 33n.)

189. See Gruss, *Jehovah's Witnesses and Prophetic Speculation* (Nutley, NJ: Presbyterian and Reformed Publishing Company, 1989), Appendix A, p. 113.

190. See Note 192, under Roy Goodrich.

191. For primary documentation consult Martin, *Jehovah of the Watchtower,* pp. 19-23; Gruss, *Apostles of Denial,* pp. 27, 45, 294-95; Gruss, *Jehovah's Witnesses and Prophetic Speculation,* chapter 6; Hoekema, *Four Major Cults,* p. 243; Van Baalen, *Chaos,* p. 259; Gruss, *We Left Jehovah's Witnesses,* op. cit., pp. 7, 65-66, 70, 74-75, 80-81, 83, 111, 118-19, 129; Montague, "Watchtower Congregations"; Hesselgrave, *Dynamic,* p. 183. For problems on the high incidents of mental illness among Jehovah's Witnesses, see Dr. Jerry Bergman, *The Mental Health of Jehovah's Witnesses* (Clayton, CA: Witness, Inc., 1987).

192. William and Joan Cetnar, *Questions for Jehovah's Witnesses* (Kunkleton, PA: Christian Literature Crusade, 1983), p. 53 (cf. pp. 48-55). The Johannes Greber translation is cited in, e.g., *Make Sure of All Things,* p. 489. Greber was a spirit medium who claimed his translation originated in the spirit world. It translates John 1:1; Hebrews 1:8, and other passages the way the NWT does. Roy Goodrich, head of the Jehovah's Witness splinter sect Back to the Bible Way, discusses the Society's involvement with psychometry and radionics in his "Demonism and the Watchtower." These are spiritistic forms of medical diagnosis. See John Weldon and Zola Levitt, *Psychic Healing,* pp. 53-65. The last known address of Back to the Bible Way was 517 N.E. Second St., Ft. Lauderdale, FL 33301.

193. Rutherford, *Riches* (WBTS, 1936), p. 316, and *Vindication* (WBTS, 1932), vol. 3, p. 250; (Rutherford, *Preparation*, 1933 pp. 36-37, 64; B.J. Kotwall and B. Stett, "Flashes of Light," (<www.watchtowerinformationservice.org/flashes.html>).

194. William and Joan Cetnar, *Questions*, p. 55.

195. Rutherford, *Preparation*, pp. 35-38, 67.

196. *Watchtower*, April 1, 1972, p. 200; cf. Sept. 1, 1932, p. 263.

197. Much of this information was supplied by Duane Magnani of Witness, Inc., P.O. Box 597, Clayton, CA 94517. For further information and documentation as to the Society's claim to direction and guidance from the spirit world, see Witness, Inc.'s tape "Angels of the New Light" and the text *The Heavenly Weatherman* (p. 3). A free catalogue of materials may be requested.

198. Gruss, *Apostles of Denial*, p. 32.

199. Ibid., pp. 15-16.

200. *Revelation—Its Grand Climax At Hand!*, 1989, p. 125 (<www.watchtowerinformationservice.org/occult.html>).

201. See the Authors' Note at the beginning of the book for additional documentation.

202. See <www.Jehovahs-Witness.com>.

203. See our book *The Facts on the Jehovah's Witnesses* (Eugene, OR: Harvest House, 2003); also Gruss discusses each of these, see his *The Jehovah's Witnesses and Prophetic Speculation* (Nutley, NJ: Presbyterian and Reformed, 1972).

204. Benjamin Wilson, *The Emphatic Diaglott New Testament* (Interlinear Edition, Brooklyn: Watchtower Bible and Tract Society, 1942), pp. 106, 372.

205. Gruss, *Apostles*, pp. 194-96.

206. Wilson, *Emphatic Diaglott*, "Preface," p. 3.

207. "How Can You Find the True Religion?" Lesson 13, point 4, emphasis in original (<www.watchtower.org/library/rg/article_13.html>).

208. Gruss, pp. 32-33, 219. See also *Watchtower*, September 1, 1932, p. 263; *Light*, Vol. 1, 1930, pp. 106, 120, 218; Vol. 2, 1930, pp. 12, 20; *Vindication*, Vol. 3, 1932, p. 250, *Preparation*, 1933, pp. 36, 67.

209. For documentation, see Cetnar and Cetnar, *Questions*, pp. 48-55.

210. See Robert M. Bowman Jr., 4-part series on Jehovah's Witnesses and the Bible, see especially parts 1 & 2, *Christian Research Journal*, Fall 1989, taken from Internet copy part 2, p. 1.

211. *The Kingdom Interlinear Translation of the Greek Scriptures* (Brooklyn: WBTS, 1969), p. 5.

212. *The New World Translation of the Holy Scriptures* (Brooklyn: WBTS, 1961), p. 5.

213. *All Scripture Is Inspired by God and Beneficial* (Brooklyn: WBTS, 1963), pp. 226-30.

214. Robert Countess, *The Jehovah's Witnesses New Testament* (Phillipsburg, NJ: Presbyterian and Reformed, 1983), pp. 91, 93.

215. Gruss, pp. 236-37.

216. Hoekema, pp. 238-39.

217. Martin, pp. 129, 175-78, cf. Gruss, p. 198.

218. Bruce Metzger, "The Jehovah's Witnesses and Jesus Christ," report of April 1953, *Theology Today* (Princeton, NJ: Theological Book Agency, 1953), p. 74.

219. Julius Mantey, *Depth Exploration in the New Testament* (New York: Vantage Press, 1980), pp. 136-37.

220. "The Royal Shepherd of Bible Prophecy," *Watchtower*, Vol. 100, no. 17, Sept. 1, 1979 (Brooklyn: WBTS), p. 30.

221. *Watchtower*, March 15, 1972, p. 189.

222. Colin Brown, *The New International Dictionary of New Testament Theology* (Grand Rapids, MI: Zondervan, 1973), Vol. 3, "Punishment"; R.C. Trench, *Synonyms of the New Testament* (Grand Rapids, MI: Eerdmans, 1978), pp. 24-25.

223. Mantey, *Depth*, p. 142.

224. Trench, *Synonyms*, pp. 25-26.

225. Mantey, *Depth*, p. 137.

226. Michael Van Buskirk, *The Scholastic Dishonesty of the Watchtower* (Santa Ana, CA: Christian Apologetics and Research Information Service, 1976).

227. Ibid.

228. Mantey, *Depth,* pp. 142-43.

229. R.C.H. Lenski, *The Interpretations of St. Luke's Gospel* (Minneapolis: Augsburg Publishers House, 1961), pp. 1145-46.

230. Martin, *Jehovah of the Watchtower,* p. 135.

231. *The Kingdom Interlinear Translation of the Greek Scriptures,* p. 1160.

232. Nigel Turner, *Grammatical Insights into the New Testament* (Edinburgh: T. and T. Clarke, 1965), pp. 14-15.

233. *The Kingdom Interlinear Translation,* p. 1160.

234. Turner, *Grammatical,* p. 15.

235. Thomas Hewitt, in the Tyndale's New Testament Commentary Series, *The Epistle to the Hebrews* (Grand Rapids, MI: Eerdmans, 1973), pp. 56-57.

236. F.F. Bruce, *The Epistle to the Hebrews* in *The New International Commentary of the New Testament* (Grand Rapids, MI: Eerdmans, 1973), p. 20.

237. *Make Sure of All Things; Hold Fast to That Which Is Fine,* p. 364.

238. Metzger, "Jehovah's Witnesses and Jesus Christ," p. 77; also Kenneth Wuest, *Word Studies in the Greek New Testament,* Vol. 2, "Hebrews" (Grand Rapids, MI: Eerdmans, 1971), p. 46.

239. A.T. Robertson, *Word Pictures in the New Testament,* Vol. 4 (Nashville: Broadman, 1930), p. 491.

240. Metzger, "Jehovah's Witnesses and Jesus Christ," pp. 77-78.

241. Gruss, *Apostles,* pp. 204-05.

242. From a condensation of Kuehne's article published in the CARIS newsletter May 1978, Vol. 2, no. 2, stated to be accurate by Kuehne in Vol. 2, no. 3, "letters."

243. Metzger, "Jehovah's Witnesses and Jesus Christ," p. 79.

244. Dana and Mantey, *A Manual Grammar of the Greek New Testament* (Toronto, Canada: MacMillian, 1957), p. 147.

245. James White, *The King James Only Controversy* (Minneapolis: Bethany, 1995), p. 270.

246. Mantey, *Depth,* pp. 138-39.

247. A.T. Robertson, *A Grammar of the Greek New Testament* (Nashville: Broadman Press, 1934), pp. 767-68.

248. A.T. Robertson, *Word Pictures,* Vol. 5, pp. 4-5.

249. Metzger, "Jehovah's Witnesses and Jesus Christ," pp. 75-76.

250. Van Buskirk, *Scholastic Dishonesty,* p. 16.

251. Countess, chapter 4, pp. 54-55, Appendix Table 5.

252. Martin, *Jehovah of the Watchtower,* p. 136.

253. Ibid., p. 141.

254. J.H. Thayer, *New Thayer's Greek-English Lexicon* (Wilmington, DE: Associated Publishers and Authors, 1977), p. 490.

255. Countess, *Jehovah's Witnesses New Testament,* p. 23; Gruss, *Apostles,* pp. 198-99.

256. Gruss, *Apostles,* pp. 198-200; Martin, *Jehovah of the Watchtower,* pp. 129-31.

257. Bruce Metzger, *The Bible Translator,* July 1964, p. 152, cited in Gruss, *Apostles,* p. 200.

258. Gruss, *Apostles,* pp. 200-05.

259. Ibid., p. 201.

260. Countess, *Jehovah's Witnesses New Testament,* ch. 6.

261. Rowley, "How Not to Translate the Bible," *The Expository Times,* Nov. 1953, pp. 41-42, cf. Jan. 1956, p. 107; cited by Gruss, *Apostles of Denial,* pp. 212-13.

262. Gruss, *Apostles,* p. 213.

263. *Watchtower,* March 1, 1975, p. 151.

264. *Aid to Bible Understanding,* pp. 1344, 1346.

265. Ibid., p. 1347.

266. Ibid., p. 1348.

267. Ibid.

268. *Watchtower,* September 1, 1979, p. 29.

269. Franz, *Crisis of Conscience* (1993), p. 138.

270. *Holy Spirit, The Force Behind the Coming New Order,* pp. 148, 150.

271. *Watchtower,* May 1, 1914, reprints, Vol. 12, p. 5450.

272. N.H. Barbour and C.T. Russell, *Three Worlds and the Harvest of this World* (1877), p. 17, cited in Gruss, *Jehovah's Witnesses and Prophetic Speculation,* p. 82.

273. C.T. Russell, *The Time Is at Hand* (1889), p. 101, cited in Gruss, *Jehovah's Witnesses and Prophetic Speculation,* p. 83.

274. *Watchtower* reprints, Vol. 4, p. 1677.

275. C.T. Russell, *The New Creation* (1904), p. 579, cited in Gruss, *Jehovah's Witnesses' and Prophetic Speculation,* p. 84.

276. *The Watchtower* reprints Vol. 6, p. 5450, cited in Gruss, *Jehovah's Witnesses and Prophetic Speculation,* p. 84.

277. Gruss, *Jehovah's Witnesses and Prophetic Speculation,* pp. 23-26.

278. *From Paradise Lost to Paradise Regained* (1958), p. 170.

279. C.T. Russell, *Thy Kingdom Come* (1891), p. 126, cited in Gruss, *Jehovah's Witnesses and Prophetic Speculation,* p. 21.

280. See Charles T. Russell, *Studies in the Scriptures,* Vol. 3, (1891), p. 284; cf. Gruss, *Apostles of Denial,* pp. 232-34.

281. C.T. Russell, *The Time Is at Hand* (1899), pp. 76-78, cited in Gruss, *Jehovah's Witnesses and Prophetic Speculation,* p. 23.

282. *Watchtower* reprints, Vol. 12, p. 5659.

283. Ibid., p. 5950.

284. Gruss, *Jehovah's Witnesses and Prophetic Speculation,* pp. 24-25.

285. *Watchtower* reprints, Vol. 9, p. 4067.

286. *Watchtower* reprints, Vol. 9, (1907), p. 4067.

287. Gruss, *Jehovah's Witnesses and Prophetic Speculation,* pp. 85-86.

288. C.J. Woodsworth and G.H. Fisher (eds.), *The Finished Mystery* (1917).

289. Gruss, *Jehovah's Witnesses and Prophetic Speculation,* pp. 85-86.

290. See Rutherford's *Millions Now Living Will Never Die* (1920), pp. 97, 105, 140, and Gruss, *Jehovah's Witnesses and Prophetic Speculation,* p. 87.

291. *Watchtower,* January 1, 1925, p. 3.

292. *Watchtower,* September, 1925, p. 262.

293. Rutherford, *Vindication* (1931), pp. 338-39, cited in Gruss, *Jehovah's Witnesses and Prophetic Speculation,* p. 89.

294. J.F. Rutherford, *Light,* Vol. 2, p. 327 (1930), cited in Gruss, *Jehovah's Witnesses and Prophetic Speculation,* p. 89.

295. J.F. Rutherford, *Vindication,* Vol. 1 (1931), p. 147.

296. J.F. Rutherford, *Preparation* (1933), p. 341.

297. Ibid., pp. 348-49.

298. Rutherford, *Vindication,* p. 310, cited in Gruss, *Jehovah's Witnesses and Prophetic Speculation,* p. 89.

299. *Let God Be True* (1946), p. 194, cited in Gruss, *Jehovah's Witnesses and Prophetic Speculation,* p. 92.

300. *This Means Everlasting Life* (1950), p. 311, cited in Gruss, *Jehovah's Witnesses and Prophetic Speculation,* p. 93.

301. *You May Survive Armageddon,* p. 11; cf. p. 362.

302. Gruss, *Jehovah's Witnesses and Prophetic Speculation,* p. 93.

303. *You May Survive Armageddon,* p. 331.

304. *From Paradise Lost,* p. 205.

305. *Your Will Be Done on Earth,* p. 105.

306. *God's Kingdom of a Thousand Years Has Approached,* p. 363; cf. pp. 24, 14, 18-21, 28, 332, 336-63.

307. *All Scripture Is Inspired by God and Beneficial* (1963), p. 286, cited in Gruss, *Jehovah's Witnesses and Prophetic Speculation,* p. 93.

308. Gruss, *Jehovah's Witnesses and Prophetic Speculation,* p. 59.

309. *Life Everlasting*, pp. 27, 29-30. As if to cover itself, the *Watchtower* of August 15, 1968, p. 494, warned against looking to 1975.
310. *Man's Salvation Out of World Distress at Hand*, p. 312.
311. Ibid., p. 369.
312. Ibid., p. 371.
313. *God's Kingdom*, p. 361.
314. *Man's Salvation Out of World Distress at Hand*, pp. 283-84.
315. Ibid., p. 366.
316. Ibid., p. 309, emphasis added.
317. Ibid., p. 308.
318. Gruss, *Jehovah's Witnesses and Prophetic Speculation*, pp. 99-101.
319. Ibid., p. 100.
320. 1975 *Yearbook*, pp. 74-75.
321. *Man's Salvation*, p. 287.
322. Russell, *Studies in the Scriptures*, Vol. 4, p. 621.
323. Eric and Jean Grieshaber, *Exposé of Jehovah's Witnesses* (1978), p. 14.
324. 1975 *Yearbook*, p. 76.
325. Rutherford, *Millions Now Living Will Never Die*, pp. 89-90, cited in Gruss, *Apostles of Denial*, p. 26.
326. 1975 *Yearbook*, pp. 145-46.
327. Ibid., pp. 74-75.
328. Gruss, *We Left Jehovah's Witnesses*, p. 20.
329. Ibid., p. 44.
330. Gruss, *Apostles of Denial*, p. 104n; cf. pp. 56-66, 76.
331. Van Baalen, *Chaos of the Cults*, p. 258.
332. Ibid., pp. 228-29.
333. Gruss, *Apostles of Denial*, pp. 19, 33.
334. Ibid., pp. 19-37.
335. Ibid., p. 234n.
336. *Watchtower*, January 15, 1969, p. 51.
337. *God's Kingdom*, p. 346.
338. Cited in Gruss, *Apostles of Denial*, p. 62n.
339. Cf. Gruss, *Apostles of Denial*, Appendix A; for example, see the April 1979 issue of *Dawn: A Herald of Christ's Presence*, pp. 41-48.
340. Van Buskirk, *Scholastic Dishonesty*, p. 24.
341. *Zion's Watch Tower*, March 1, 1896, p. 47; cf. *Studies in the Scriptures*, Vol. 4, pp. 613-14; *Zion's Watch Tower*, April 15, 1904, p. 125; *Watchtower*, March 1, 1923, p. 68, cited in Van Buskirk, *Scholastic Dishonesty*, pp. 27-42.
342. Van Buskirk, *Scholastic Dishonesty*, p. 32.
343. Duane Magnani, *Who Is the Faithful and Wise Servant?* (Clayton, CA: Witness, 1992), pp. 31-32.
344. Martin, *Jehovah of the Watchtower*, pp. 41-42.
345. Ibid., pp. 21-24, 36, 41-42.
346. Rutherford, *Vindication*, 1931, cited in Gruss, *Apostles of Denial*, p. 57.
347. Rutherford, *Preparation*, p. 343.
348. Gruss, *Apostles of Denial*, pp. 57, 59.
349. Ibid., p. 57.
350. *Watchtower*, July 15, 1960, p. 439.
351. *Studies in the Scriptures*, vol. 7, p. 159.
352. *Then Is Finished the Mystery of God*, p. 232.
353. Rutherford, *Reconciliation*, pp. 323-24.
354. Rutherford, *Salvation*, p. 43.
355. *From Paradise Lost to Paradise Regained*, p. 236.

356. C.T. Russell, *Studies in the Scriptures*, Vol. 1, p. 110.

357. *Watchtower*, February 1, 1954, p. 85.

358. *Watchtower*, March 1, 1965, p. 139.

359. *Watchtower* reprints, July 15, 1898, p. 2337.

360. *Watchtower* reprints, October 1880, p. 144.

361. Charter of the Watchtower Society of Pennsylvania, Article II.

362. *Watchtower*, January 1, 1954, p. 31.

363. *Watchtower*, May 15, 1954, p. 317.

364. Russell, *Studies in the Scriptures*, Vol. 5, p. 478.

365. J.F. Rutherford, *The Harp of God*, pp. 328 or 334, depending on edition.

366. Russell, *Studies in the Scriptures*, Vol. 5, pp. 478-86.

367. Rutherford, *Salvation*, p. 224.

368. Russell, *Studies in the Scriptures*, Vol. 3, p. 244.

369. Rutherford, *Comfort for the Jews*, p. 55.

370. *Let God be True*, 2nd ed., pp. 217-18.

371. Russell, *Studies in the Scriptures*, Vol. 1, p. 266.

372. *This Means Everlasting Life*, p. 197.

373. *Babylon the Great Has Fallen! God's Kingdom Rules!* p. 548.

374. *What Pastor Russell Said*, p. 297.

375. Rutherford, *Vindication*, Vol. 3, p. 204.

376. Rutherford, *Riches*, pp. 324-25.

377 Rutherford, *Prophecy*, pp. 67-68.

378. *Awake!* March 22, 1963, p. 32.

379. Gruss, *Apostles of Denial*, p. 255.

380. Van Buskirk, *Scholastic Dishonesty*, p. 47.

381. Gruss, *Apostles of Denial*, p. 193.

382. Ibid., p. 107.

383. Ibid., pp. 107-08.

384. Gruss, *Jehovah's Witnesses and Prophetic Speculation*, ch. 3.

385. Ibid., p. 37.

386. Van Buskirk, *Scholastic Dishonesty*, p. 15.

387. Ibid. The xeroxed reproduction of the Westcott and Hort Text (p. v) is from James White, *The King James Only Controversy* (Minneapolis: Bethany, 1995), citing Robertson, *The Minister and His Greek New Testament*, p. 62.

388. William Barclay, *Many Witnesses, One Lord* (1963), pp. 23-24.

389. Ibid., p. 23.

390. Ibid., p. 24.

391. Colin Brown (ed.), *The New International Dictionary of New Testament Theology* (1977), pp. 81-82.

392. Ibid., p. 82.

393. As far as we can determine, this practice has not been discontinued.

394. Van Buskirk, *Scholastic Dishonesty*, p. 7.

395. Ibid., pp. 12-13.

396. See, e.g., the *New World Translation* 1953 appendix, pp. 770-71 and the original *Britannica* article edition 11, Vol. 7, p. 506; *The New Catholic Encyclopedia*, 1967, Vol. 14, p. 306 with *The Truth that Leads to Eternal Life*, 1968, p. 22; *The Quarterly Journal*, July-Sept. 1990, p. 10.

397. For primary documentation consult Martin, *Jehovah of the Watchtower*; Gruss, *Apostles of Denial*, pp. 27, 45, 294-95; Gruss, *Jehovah's Witnesses and Prophetic Speculation*, ch. 6; Hoekema, *Four Major Cults*, p. 243; Van Baalen, *Chaos*, p. 259; Gruss, *We Left Jehovah's Witnesses*, pp. 7, 65-66, 70, 74-75, 80-81, 83, 111, 118-19, 129; H. Montague, *Watchtower Congregations—Communion or Conflict: An Inside Look at the Kingdom Hall*; published by CARIS; and Hesselgrave, *Dynamic Religious Movements*, p. 183.

398. Martin, *Jehovah of the Watchtower*, p. 21.

399. Gruss, *We Left Jehovah's Witnesses*, p. 7.

400. Ibid., p. 66.

401. H. Montague, *Watchtower Congregations—Communion or Conflict: An Inside Look at the Kingdom Hall*, published by CARIS.

402. Gruss, *We Left Jehovah's Witnesses*, pp. 118-19.

403. Montague, *Jehovah's Witnesses and Blood Transfusions.*

404. Gruss, *We Left Jehovah's Witnesses*, p. 66

405. Montague, *Jehovah's Witnesses and Blood Transfusions*, p. 19.

406. *Awake!* March 8, 1960, p. 27.

407. *Christianity Today,* December 12, 1980, p. 69.

408. John Stedman, "Jehovah's Witnesses and Mental Illness," *CARIS Newsletter,* February-March, 1977; Vol. 1, no. 2.

409. Ibid.

410. Ibid.

411. Jerry Bergman, "Paradise Postponed...And Postponed: Why Jehovah's Witnesses Have a High Mental Illness Level," *Christian Research Journal,* Summer 1976, pp. 36-37, 41. See especially Lois Randel, "The Apocalypticism of the Jehovah's Witnesses," *Free Inquiry,* Winter 1984, pp. 18-24, as well as *The British Journal of Psychiatry,* June 1975; *Social Compass,* March 1976; *The American Journal of Psychiatry,* March 1949; Robert Potter, "A Social Psychological Study of Fundamentalist Christianity" (Ph.D. Dissertation, Sussex University, England, 1985); and Kjell Totland, "The Mental Health of Jehovah's Witnesses," *Journal of the Norwegian Psychological Association,* 1996.

412. Morey, *How to Answer a Jehovah's Witness*, pp. 14-15.

413. See, e.g., *Watchtower,* June, 1906, from Gerstner, *The Theology of the Major Sects,* p. 34.

414. *Aid to Understanding the Bible,* p. 500.

415. Hoekema, *Four Major Cults,* p. 332.

416. Gruss, *We Left Jehovah's Witnesses,* p. 21.

417. Gruss, *Apostles of Denial,* pp. 261-63.

418. The verses listed with each of these five points should be read in a good, modern translation like the New International Version or the New American Standard Bible, because some were mistranslated in the King James Version and in the *New World Translation.*

419. Metzger, *The Bible Translator,* pp. 79-80.

420. Moulton and Milligan, *The Vocabulary of the Greek Testament* (1980), p. 683. See F.F. Bruce, *The Epistle to the Hebrews; The New International Commentary on the New Testament* (1973), pp. 5-6.

421. M.J. Schnell, *Jehovah's Witnesses' Errors Exposed,* pp. 13; cf. p. 100.

422. *Is This Life All There Is?* p. 99.

423. Franz, *Crisis of Conscience,* p. 31.

424. *Is This Life All There Is?* p. 99.

OTHER BOOKS BY
JOHN ANKERBERG AND JOHN WELDON

Fast Facts™ on Islam
Fast Facts™ on Defending Your Faith
Fast Facts™ on False Teachings
Fast Facts™ on Jehovah's Witnesses
Fast Facts™ on Mormonism
What Do Mormons Really Believe?

The Facts on Angels
The Facts on Creation vs. Evolution
The Facts on Halloween
The Facts on Homosexuality
The Facts on Islam
The Facts on the Jehovah's Witnesses
The Facts on the King James Only Debate
The Facts on the Masonic Lodge
The Facts on the Mormon Church
The Facts on the New Age Movement
The Facts on the Occult
The Facts on Roman Catholicism